MY MOTHER'S CURSE

Ozone Park. Queens, New York 1957

Wheaton, Illinois 1973

12/24/19

...+ Brenda, ...can never adequately express ...importance of your ...presence and the ...batchelor family in my ...life journey. Hopefully this ...book will help just a bit. With deep love & gratitude, Christine

MY MOTHER'S CURSE

A Journey Beyond Childhood Trauma

Christine Nicolette-Gonzalez

LAUREATE
LIFE PRESS

Dallas

MY MOTHER'S CURSE: A Journey Beyond Childhood Trauma

To contact the author, visit www.laureatelifepress.com.

Cover Design: The Shop | theshopagency.com
Cover Illustration: Mark Ross

Library of Congress Control Number: 2019918912

ISBN 978-0-578-61088-7

For my children and grandchildren
with hope that you will always find light
even in the inevitable darkness.

I've always practiced what I've encouraged my students to do—
to write throughout their lives.
Since I was ten years old, I've written poetry
and kept numerous journals.
The poetry in this memoir comes directly from these journals.
The letters, lists, journal entries, and poems
were written on their depicted dates.

Someday you are going to write about this, Christine,
and what a story it will be.

—Charles S. Nicolette

My mother died more than twenty-four years ago, and it has taken me this long to have the emotional strength to write this memoir. I have tried so many times. When we bought Casa Verde in 2010, I thought that our mountain retreat would be the perfect place to write; I was wrong. Often while we were there, I would pick up my pen and begin to write a vignette or two...and then stop. It was simply too difficult to return to the trauma of my childhood. But recently, I had a realization that overpowered my pain. If my experience could help other people understand and better deal with their own childhood trauma, I had to find the courage to tell this story.

In late May of 2019, I heard a knocking that I had to answer. It was finally time to open the door.

May 1938

After an agonizingly long winter, the sun is finally out and shining brightly in Brooklyn, New York. A handsome, Italian young man is waiting on a tennis court in Prospect Park for his friend to show up so they can hit a few balls. While waiting, he sees a young woman arrive carrying a tennis racquet and a can of tennis balls. The first thing the young man notices are her piercing blue eyes that have an intensity unlike anything he has ever seen. She takes a seat on a nearby bench and acknowledges him with a nod.

He waits for about fifteen minutes with his racquet in his hand. Finally, he decides that his friend must have forgotten about their tennis plans, so as he begins to leave the court, he crosses by the young woman who is still sitting on the bench.

"Have you been stood up, too?" he asks her with a slight grin.

"I guess so."

"Well, since we both would like to get a little exercise, would you like to hit a few balls?"

"Sure."

They walk to their places on both sides of the tennis court and begin to volley.

"So what is your name?"

"Sophie Pines. Yours?"

Salvatore Nicoletti looks at the woman's round face, wavy brown hair, blue eyes, and sturdy, shapely body. She reminds him of some of the Jewish girls he knew at Erasmus Hall where he had attended high school.

"Charlie Bernstein," he replies.

Charlie and Sophie begin to date. After a few months of enjoying meals at restaurants, dancing, and watching a few movies at the theater, he invites her to join him for a trip to Jones Beach on the south shore of Long Island. This is a place that Sophie has heard so much about but has never been, so she quickly accepts his invitation.

Later that day as they are standing in the sand by the billowing waves, he turns to her and says, "There is something that I need to tell you. I haven't been honest with you because I was afraid if you knew the truth, you wouldn't want to see me anymore. My name isn't Charlie Bernstein. It's Salvatore Nicoletti. And I'm not Jewish. I'm Italian and Catholic."

At first, Sophie is so angry with his dishonesty that she thinks about telling him that their relationship is over and to take her back home. But she really enjoys spending time with him, and she also knows that at the age of twenty-two, she sure isn't getting any younger. Just about every girl she knows of her age is already married, and there isn't anyone else of the opposite sex in her Jewish community whom she is even remotely interested in. So she tells him that he better not ever lie to her about anything again and agrees to keep seeing him.

But what should she tell her parents? The worst thing a Jewish girl can do is to marry someone outside her faith…especially someone from a large, "dirty" Italian family. But her parents already have met Charlie, and even though he is nine years older than their daughter, they like him because he is so kind and generous. Despite his age, they are happy that their daughter is finally dating an eligible young Jewish man and that she might not end up being an "old maid" after all. Sophie decides to wait to tell her parents and to keep calling him Charlie.

Their courtship moves slowly as Charlie isn't a fan of cigarettes, and he can't seem to convince Sophie to stop smoking. He wants to enjoy the kisses they share, but with her cigarette breath, he isn't always in the mood to kiss her. There is also something different about Sophie, something that he hasn't ever seen in any other woman he has dated—and there have been quite a few of these women. Sophie is very private about her life. He hasn't ever heard her talk about any of her friends. It appears that most of her free time is spent at home with her mother Esther, a homemaker, and with her father Ike, a carpenter. She did tell him that both of her parents had immigrated to the United States from Kiev, Russia, in the late 1800s.

After dating on and off for a few years, one night Charlie gets a call from Sophie. She tells him her mother had a heart attack and four days ago was admitted to Kings County Hospital in Brooklyn. Sophie is spending every day and night with her mother, so if he wants to see her, he needs to come to the hospital.

When Charlie visits her a few days later, the first thing he sees is a transformation in Sophie's face. While most people in her situation would be worried about their mom's health and be distraught, Sophie seems to have a renewed and upbeat spirit.

She greets him with enthusiasm and tells him she is certain that her mom's illness is for a good reason, and because she and others have been praying to God for her mom's health, she is confident that her mom will be healed.

God? When has he ever heard her mention God? How could she be this happy when her mom is still lying in bed breathing very shallowly while the doctors are trying to figure out what is wrong with her heart?

Charlie stays with Sophie for a while and then asks her if she has eaten dinner. She hasn't. He suggests that they grab a bite to eat at the hospital cafeteria. They head down the four flights of stairs and find themselves facing each other over chicken salad sandwiches, tossed green salads, apple pie, and coffee. He must find out what has caused this change in Sophie.

When Charlie asks Sophie about her new God-talk, she tells him that on the night when her mother was admitted to the hospital, she was resting by her mom's side when there was a knock at the door. When she opened it, she saw a kind-looking man who told her he was from the American Seminary of the Bible and asked if she had a few minutes to talk. Since she had been feeling quite lonely before the knock, she invited him in.

He introduced himself as Reverend John Kline, a chaplain from the seminary, and he asked if he could pray with her for her mom to be healed. While Sophie was raised in the Jewish faith, she hadn't attended services at the synagogue for quite a while. But she remembered listening to many prayers in Hebrew when she was younger. What harm would it do to pray?

John began to pray out loud for her mother in a confident and passionate voice—almost like he was talking to God directly. She had never heard anyone pray like this and was taken aback by his sincerity and concern for someone he didn't even know. When she heard his "Amen," she opened her eyes to see great kindness and compassion in John's eyes.

He asked her if she had ever read the New Testament before, and she told him that she hadn't. He took out a pocket-sized book titled *Old Testament Prophesy Edition of the New Testament* on its navy cover and told Sophie he wanted her to have it. He told her that this book cited all the passages of the New Testament that were the fulfillment of the prophecies of the coming to Earth of the Messiah that the Old Testament predicted—in other words, passages that revealed that Jesus Christ was the Messiah that the Jews were still waiting for.

That night when her mom was finally asleep, Sophie found herself unable to sleep. With the words of John's prayer still in her head, she opened the small New Testament and began to read. She was mesmerized by the stories of Jesus that were retold in each of the Gospels, and she couldn't put the book down. In each account of Jesus' birth, she saw in the margins corresponding verses from the Old Testament that had foretold that this event would happen. She kept reading.

Before she knew it, she was at a book titled John. It was in chapter three that she read a verse that she had seen in public places before: John 3:16. She read that God had sent his Son to the world, and if she simply believed in that Son, she could be saved and have everlasting life. Wouldn't it be amazing if her mom could have everlasting life? It sounded too good to be true.

Now, Something was moving her to do this. She got out of her chair and fell to her knees like she had seen the rabbis do at her family's synagogue. And she prayed a very simple prayer: "God, I accept your Son Jesus as my Savior." Then she went back to her chair and quickly joined her mom in a deep sleep.

The next morning, she woke to bright sunlight flooding the hospital room. She found her mom more lucid than she had been in days. More than anything, Sophie was overcome with a huge wave of joy; she knew that beyond a doubt, her prayer to God last night was heard, and God was now real to her in a way that He had never been before.

A few hours later, after the doctors came to check on her mom, and her mom fell back to sleep, Sophie opened the New Testament once more. Inside the cover she found a phone number for American Seminary of the Bible. She really wanted to talk to someone about what she had experienced the previous night, so she walked out of the hospital room to a phone at the end of the hall and dialed the number.

A young man answered. She introduced herself and told him about meeting John Kline and that she had accepted Jesus Christ as her Messiah. He sounded so pleased to hear this and invited her to attend a Bible study at the seminary the following night.

Even though she wouldn't know anyone at this meeting except John, she knew that she had been feeling very isolated lately and decided to leave her mom at the hospital to attend it. What a great decision that was! She was quickly surrounded by the kindest group of people she had ever met, and they all seemed so interested in hearing her conversion story. They had never met anyone of the Jewish faith who had accepted the Messiah simply by reading the New Testament. The leader of the Bible study talked about how Christians should put on the armor of Christ. They are to put away their worldly clothes and lifestyles and to wear pure clothes and to live pure lives that honor Christ.

Sophie thought about the many things she did that showed that she was living in the world and wasn't as pure as Christ wanted her to be: she smoked, she occasionally drank alcohol, she wore makeup, and sometimes she went out dancing and to the theatre. She vowed right then and there to change into her new armor of purity like that worn by the many Christian people who surrounded her.

Charlie listens carefully to every word Sophie says. He sees that she isn't wearing her usual lipstick, and her breath doesn't smell of cigarettes like it usually does. Before he leaves the hospital for the night, Sophie invites him to attend a service at the Norwegian Hospital in Brooklyn on Saturday night. Dr. G. P. Raud, the president of the seminary, was conducting a service for patients, nurses, and doctors and had asked Sophie to give her testimony of salvation. Charlie is intrigued. He is growing to love this woman, so he decides he'd better show up.

Saturday night comes, and Sophie and Charlie make their way to the service. After the opening prayer and a few hymns, John introduces Sophie to a large group of several hundred people. Charlie can't believe what he is seeing. This demure introvert is confidently walking up to the podium! In a few minutes, everyone in the room is spellbound with her story, including Charlie. He must learn more; he wants what she has.

After the service, Charlie speaks to John and tells him that he has strayed far from his Catholic upbringing and wants to begin a new life as a Christian. He knows he has sinned a great deal in the past, and he is willing to change his lifestyle like Sophie has done.

A couple of months later, Charlie and Sophie decide that God clearly brought them together as a couple whose main goal in life is to serve the Lord. In a small service at the American Seminary of the Bible, Dr. Raud marries them on February 7, 1942. Since they both are marrying outside their faiths, their union is difficult for both of their families; only Sophie's father, Ike Pines, attends the wedding.

Not long after, despite having a high draft number and being in his mid-thirties, Charlie is called to serve as an officer in the army. With Sophie now twenty-six years of age, and Charlie thirty-five, they had planned to quickly have a son named Paul who would join them in their joint mission to serve the Lord. But now that plan is put on hold.

To: Charles S. Nicolette
The United States Army
Bougainville, The Solomon Islands

May 11, 1944

My Lover,

I hope you are over the spell of lovesickness you had a while ago. Rest assured that when you get back you are going to get an ample supply of hugs, kisses, tight squeezes, and all other forms of love just as we know how to engage in. So please be contented to just live for the future for a while. Look at all the good it's doing to you, too. After this separation, my ears shall never hear again the desire on your part to go somewhere without me, shall never hear again wanting to eat outside your home or wanting to go to places of worldly interest without me. The Lord is purging you through all of this, and I pray you are taking it all in good grace.

You are soon going to be released and then you are going to be the best husband in the whole world--and I'm going to be the best wife. Darling, we have much to look ahead to and we are going to have a most fruitful life in Christ. We've going to attain that perfection of Christian life where never a bad word will leave our lips, where never a bad thought will come into our minds, and where our hearts will be filled with love for everyone.

Yes, dear. I want an ideal life together as He Himself desires when He looks down upon us. A house divided in itself cannot stand. And dear, you must admit that there were too many divisions between us. Well that's in the past and it will be different from now on. You've said that before and it was just the same.

Charlie, I want you to give the Lord your very word now that you are going to live right. The way I wanted you to live from the start. I want Him to come first in everything we do and that way we can never go wrong. I want a perfect unity in Christ between us. When you'll say Yes to Him. I'm sure He'll listen and give you that peace which you so need.

Love in Christ,
Sophie

August 6th, 1944

Dear Hubby,

I'm off every other Sunday now, and I was off today. Spent a quiet day at home looking over the paper and listening to my favorite gospel programs. The war news is encouraging as usual these days, and it looks like Germany will surrender very soon. Often throughout the day I pray that the Lord will bring you home very soon and while praying, I pray in prayer believing that He will do it.

You say that you just wonder how you have stood it during all this time of separation. He provides the grace to bring His children through all trials and tribulation. He is taking care of me, and I just hope and pray that by the time you come back we may both be in perfect health to do great things for Eternity.

I know that is the only way a Christian can find real happiness. You won't find it on a dance floor or in strong drink or in gambling. You won't find it at picture shows, either.

The only way is to study God's Word, know it, seek others for salvation, pray, and have fellowship with Christians. That is the only way to true happiness for a saved person.

When a child of God indulges in things of the world, he is out of fellowship with God and is mentally unstable. One has to live close to the Lord to enjoy a healthy normal Christian life. May God grant us a holy Christian life together with definite times

set aside for prayer and reading His word.
May we also save many souls for eternity.

Lovingly in Christ,
Sophie

October 8th, 1944

My loving husband,

If you were to pop in on me these days in my playground you would find your wife fitting, cutting, and sewing costumes for kids. Besides that, you might find her teaching a ballet or you might discover her as a short stop in a punch ball game. Such is the life of that bundle of love of yours. Of course, it's lots of fun, healthful, and most interesting work. But should that husband of mine pop up--ah! That would be desires gratified.

Yes, dear. I need you near me so I can read my Bible out loud and absorb what I'm reading. I need you near me because I can have my love to kiss and kiss. I need you near me because I want my husband at my side where ere I go. I need you near me so I can have my husband to dine with me. I need you near because I want my cooking appreciated. I need you near me to pray with. I need you near me to shop with. I need you near me to do things for you. I need you near me to love.

That's quite a lot of reasons for having the Army give you your orders home. Won't you please write a list of "I need you near me's?" That would gladden my heart. I suppose the first reason would be to massage your scalp. Oh well. Maybe there's some other reasons.

Love in Christ,
Sophie

November 12, 1944

My darling,

Spent an interesting afternoon today at Central Park seeing the annual children's dance pageant. The kids did fine in the sweltering heat and the playground directors felt that their hard work training them was well worth it. Next week our dance takes place, and I'm really looking forward to the occasion. I enjoyed teaching it to them immensely, and the children enjoy doing it. Our costumes are magnificent.

To think that I would ever like work of this type! As soon as you come home, I'm afraid it's going to lose all its glamour though. Yes, then I'll only be interested in making for you that ideal Christian wife and leading a close life together in Him. That's how real enjoyment of life can be had and not in the world. Of course, I'm certainly not worldly now but teaching a dance might be a bit toward that way. I've been hearing all sorts of prophecies on the radio about the war being over at the end of October in Europe. It can't come too soon for this wife. God speed that day.

Lovingly in Christ,
Sophie

December 2, 1944

Darling,

I do hope the heat of the tropics is not too severe right now. I am praying that you come home before your summer sets in. It's probably unbearable at that time.

I notice on a scale of weights that a man 5 ft. 8 inches should weigh 154 pounds. I want you to gain the necessary poundage to make this weight. You look well when you are on the chubbier side. I do want you to make a handsome picture when you return. Eat lots of butter and drink all the milk you can and maybe that will help. I know if you were in a cooler climate gaining a few pounds would be no problem.

I weighed 134 pounds today and pray that I stay there. You know I have a tendency to get fat. I'd like to weigh 130 before we get started on Paul for I do not want to be too big when I'm pregnant. And while we're on the subject of Paul, I want to inform you that I'd like to have him before I'm 30. You know that I'll be 29 in a few months so PRAY. Darling what would it be like if you were to walk in the door right now, and I'd look around and look into those eyes of yours... heaven.

Lovingly in Him,
Sophie

After World War II ends, Charlie returns home to Sophie. For eight years he and Sophie enjoy a happy, zealous Christian life as they reside in Long Island, New York. And they never stop praying for their dreamed-of son Paul to become a reality. On September 24, 1953, their prayers are finally answered when Paul Richard is born. Due to their advanced ages, Charlie and Sophie both assume that one child will be all they will ever have. But that doesn't prove to be true when almost four years later at the age of forty-one, Sophie gives birth to me, Christine Elise, on June 24, 1957, Charlie's fiftieth birthday.

My story begins five years later.

May 1962
Commack, Long Island, New York

Mother has just walked out of the kitchen where she has been making our dinner. In a few hours, Daddy will return on the Long Island Railroad from his job as a clerk in the Kings County Supreme Court in Brooklyn. It takes him two hours each way to get to his job and back home each day, but he tells me he doesn't mind the long trip because he can read the newspaper on the train, and we can live in our pretty neighborhood that is far from the busy city.

I sit on our blue living room sofa, look out the window, and wait for my daddy to get home. Mother walks over to our large bay window to join me and to check on Paul who has been riding his bike in circles around the cul-de-sac. I watch as she looks for him and then sees Mr. Grogan, our next-door neighbor, walking by our house. Mother often talks about how mean Mr. Grogan is. She even told me she had seen Mr. Grogan yell at and shake Paul because he thought Paul was bothering his son Stephen. She thinks Mr. Grogan has the devil in him.

Suddenly, Mr. Grogan stops walking and turns to stare at Paul. Then we see him stroke the hair on his head three times with his right hand. At that moment, Paul falls off his bicycle and onto the street. Paul begins to cry out in pain, and we rush out the front door to help him. Mr. Grogan says nothing and walks off.

October 1962

"I don't have to if I don't want to!"

Quickly, I learn how to talk back to my mother. She asks me to do things that I don't want to do, like get my hair cut so short that I look like a boy. I see all the girls in my class who have long, flowing hair, and I want to be pretty like them. Paul always gives in to our mother's wishes—even it if means getting his hair cut into a crew cut or wearing a bow tie to school each day and then being teased by his classmates. So Mother is never angry at him. But I don't want Mother to tell me what to do, even if she is my mother.

One day after kindergarten, she tells me I need to drink a strange drink that she just made. I had seen her put a raw egg into it. It looks disgusting.

"I don't have to if I don't want to!"

Suddenly, she comes at me. She takes my arms, and with her large body, she knocks me to the kitchen floor. I feel hard slaps to my face. Then I feel so much pain as she kicks me in my side, in my shoulder, and in my legs.

She screams, "I'm kicking all the demons out of you, Christine! You will not talk to me like this anymore!"

I try to fight back, but it is useless. She is a giant and is so much stronger than I am. I scream for my daddy and for Paul, but my daddy is still at work. Paul is still at school. My beating goes on and on; it seems like it will never end. I am crying so hard.

"Stop! Stop! I promise I'll never say that again."

She finally stops hitting and kicking me and walks away. I try to get up, but it hurts too much to move. After a few minutes pass, I raise my bruised body and slowly walk into my bedroom.

I whisper the only words I can say, "I want my daddy."

December 1962

It's snowing outside, and Mother tells me to get in the car. She needs to buy a few things at Klein's, the local department store by our home. I get into the front seat of our blue Chevrolet, and she starts up the car. I know that Mother doesn't like to drive like Daddy does, but since the store is just a few minutes away, she won't have to drive very far.

As we come closer to the intersection near the store, I see the stoplight in front of me turn red. Mother is not slowing down. I can tell she hasn't seen it.

I scream out, "Stop!"

Mother slams her foot on the brake.

It's too late. I hear a loud crashing sound and feel our car hit the other car in the intersection. The impact is great, and my head hits hard plastic. My neck goes backwards, and I feel a wave of pain. Our car has stopped moving, and I am now bent over and lying on the car floor, crying out in pain.

Mother reaches over to me and asks if I am okay. I see two people's faces looking into the window on my door. A tall man opens the door to our car and in an angry voice he yells in, "Lady, what were you thinking?"

She wasn't. By the time we arrive back home, my head still hurts so much, and when I reach up to touch it, I feel something like a ball that is now stuck to my forehead. I walk inside the house and lie down on the couch. I haven't ever felt this much pain in my head before, and the room seems to be moving around me. In the background I hear my daddy yelling at Mother. I try to block out their words as I rest on the couch. Daddy takes Mother's car keys away that night.

January 1963

We have just finished eating dinner, and it's still too cold to go outside, so we're all sitting inside in our small living room. Mother has her black Bible open and is reading quietly. Paul is reading a book, and Daddy is reading the newspaper. I'm sitting on the couch with my legs crossed, and one by one, I look at each of them reading.

"It's not fair! I want to read, too!"

Daddy looks up from the paper and motions for me to come to him. He sweeps me into his strong arms and sits me on his lap.

"Let's read this together, Christine. Look at this word. Sunday. S-U-N-D-A-Y. Can you say Sunday?"

"Sunday," I respond.

Where is the S?"

"Right there."

"And the Y?"

"There."

"See? You can read, too!"

I'm so proud of myself. I never want to leave his lap. Or stop reading.

June 1963

It's finally summer, and school is out. I'm so excited to turn six. Most of the kids in Mrs. Bernie's kindergarten class are already six, but that doesn't matter.

Today, I'm going to have a birthday party, and we have invited eight of my classmates. Because of the time she spent as a children's playground director, my mother still knows a lot of games that children play—games like "Rattlesnake," "London Bridge," and "The Farmer in the Dell." Rattlesnake is my favorite because we all get to be twisted together in one long chain and chant "R-A-T-T-L-E-S-N-A-K-E spells rattlesnake" before we slowly get so twisted that we all fall down.

This is the most excited I've ever seen Mother. She prepared for my party by buying lots of party goods. Since we have so few "worldly" toys in my house to play with, I've been staring at the party packages for days, waiting for her to open them.

She bought many crepe-papered red lanterns, and my daddy has just strung them all over the tall trees in our backyard. She also made goodie bags of little toys, including a game called Jacks that she taught me to play.

I try to get her to buy some candy to put in the bags, but she refuses because she thinks candy is junk and made from sugar that kids don't need. But I know that my friends would love to get some candy in their goodie bags.

And then, what will we do for a cake if my mother doesn't want them to eat any sugar? And what will my friends drink if they can't have Kool-Aid or lemonade or soda like they're used to drinking at parties?

Even though I'm happy that right now my mother isn't talking about demons like she often does, I'm still embarrassed by this because I want my friends to have a good time and to like me.

The party is so much fun! Mother does a great job leading all of us in the games. I never have seen her this happy or have known she could be this much fun. I love that Paul and Daddy are there, too.

After the games in our backyard, we go inside for the cake and presents. Now I realize I haven't seen my birthday cake yet. We gather around our small dining room table, and my daddy begins to pour milk into paper cups while my mother disappears into the kitchen to get the cake. Why couldn't it be chocolate milk like I've seen some of my other friends drink? Then Mother walks to our table carrying a platter that's covered with aluminum foil. She slowly lifts the foil.

Most birthday cakes I've seen have layers of icing between cake and colorful icing on top. Sometimes they even have "Happy Birthday" written on them. This cake has big strawberries on top of whipped cream. Underneath the whipped cream are two pound cakes. From the looks on their faces, my friends haven't ever seen a birthday cake like this, either.

My daddy puts six candles on the cake and lights them. I hear everyone begin to sing "Happy Birthday." I blow the candles out, and my mother asks, "Who wants a piece of birthday cake?"

Not one of my friends responds.

July 1963

On most summer nights, even though it doesn't get dark outside until 9:00 p.m., we must go to bed at 7:30 p.m. I hate leaving the yellow hammock in our backyard. When I lie in it and look up at the tall trees and sky, I always feel like I'm resting in a happy place. But I'm also happy when I go back inside the house because I know I'll be close to Paul in the bedroom we share.

Tonight, once again we aren't tired, so we lie in our beds and talk. No matter what question I ask, Paul knows the answer. And no matter what's going on outside of our bedroom, I feel safe as long as he's there lying in his bed that's so close to mine.

Once a month we're told to go to bed even earlier because there's a Bible study in our house at 7:00 p.m. On those nights, Daddy comes home from work early. He mops the kitchen floor and dusts and vacuums the living room carpet, even though Mother has been home all day long without much to do—except for reading her Bible and the books on witchcraft that she has now checked out of the library.

On Bible study nights we eat a quick dinner, and then six to eight people arrive at our house carrying black leather Bibles under their arms. Roma Bader, a tall, manly-looking woman, is among them. She always is dressed in a navy, tight-fitted suit, dark hose, and flat black shoes, and her long hair is pulled back into a tight bun. When she says hello to us, she never smiles. For a few years, she's the only friend my mother has. And then Mother decides Miss Bader is a witch like everyone else.

August 1963

Daddy gets a three-week vacation from his job every year, and his vacation time is finally here. We're headed to Quebec, Canada, to the Keswick Bible Conference because Mother tells us that we can't spend our vacation at any worldly place. We must go to a place where all four of us can learn more about the Bible.

It takes a long time for Daddy to drive us up there. The first night of our trip we stay at a motel with a swimming pool, so Daddy, Paul, and I get to swim! The next afternoon we finally arrive at a pretty place that has lots of buildings and a lake. Daddy shows us the room where we'll be sleeping and the building where there will be Bible studies every morning after breakfast and every night after dinner. We are the only kids at the conference, so we must go to the Bible studies with our parents and silently sit with them till they're over. It's so hard to do this!

I'm so happy that we have free time every afternoon. That's when Mother stays in the room reading her Bible, and Daddy takes us out to the lake to swim. We also go out in the water in a paddleboat and canoe for the first time. One afternoon, he tells me he wants to take me down the big slide that goes into the lake. I've watched Paul slide down it many times, and it looks like so much fun, so I decide to be brave and slide down it with Daddy.

We climb up the many slide stairs together. Even though Daddy is behind me, I'm still so scared. When we get to the top, I still feel him right behind me and hear him say, "Don't be afraid, Christine. Just hold on to my legs, and we'll go down together. It looks much scarier than it is."

We both sit down on the slide, and I hold on to his legs. I can see so much from way up here! He pushes off, and I feel my body move faster than it's ever moved before. We are going down, down, down, and then SPLASH! We land in the cool lake water. I feel so proud of myself!

Then I look up at Daddy. His face looks like he's in pain. Without my knowing it, to slow us down so I wouldn't be scared, Daddy had used his arms to squeeze the iron sides of the slide the entire way down. I feel so sorry for him, because now he has two long, bright red burns under both of his arms. They look like they hurt him a lot, but he doesn't say anything about them.

At the Bible study that night, once again, Paul and I use our imaginations to take us far away from this holy place.

November 1963

I'm in the first grade at Green Fields School, and a pretty, dark-haired woman named Mrs. Light is my teacher. How I love going to school! Since I spent so much time last year in my daddy's lap learning how to read, I'm one of the best readers in the class, and Mrs. Light often calls on me to read out loud. I also like gym class because I get to move and music class because I love to sing. Many days I don't want the final bell of the day to ring. I've already decided that someday I want to be a teacher. That way I can make sure that I'll go to school for the rest of my life.

Mother is still talking about demons and witches. Daddy tells me he thinks she does this because while I'm at school she spends most of her time reading books about witchcraft. He tells me not to listen to what she says—that she is just being silly. But it doesn't sound silly to me.

I see her make a lot of strange movements with her hands when she's sitting in the brown armchair in the living room. Since the day Paul fell off his bicycle, she keeps telling us that our next-door neighbor, Mr. Grogan, is a wizard, and she often talks about how evil he is. Last Saturday, when she was outside watering the plants, she saw him watering his grass, and she began to yell at him for cursing her son Paul. Even from inside the house, I could hear him yell back at her. Daddy quickly walked outside and got her to come inside.

"What is wrong with you, Sophie? You must stop this ridiculous behavior. If you don't, you're going to end up in the back of a police car!"

Besides talking about the witches and wizards around her, Mother loves to cook. She constantly talks about food and the difference between healthy food and junk food. She often tells us what she has read in a book by a woman named Adelle Davis. I hate taking my lunch to school because my lunch doesn't look like the lunch of any of the other kids in my class. All my classmates eat sandwiches made of soft, white bread, but I have sandwiches made on dark, whole-wheat bread. My friends eat bologna and salami sandwiches, but I eat tuna fish sandwiches, peanut butter, or turkey sandwiches. And they get little bags of potato chips and chocolate-chip cookies! I only get a piece of fruit for dessert. I can never drink from juice boxes—only from milk cartons. I want so much to eat what my friends eat. Their food looks so much better than mine.

When I get home from school, my snack is applesauce with cottage cheese. Cooking dinner for us is the only house chore we ever see Mother do, and she lets us know how hard she has worked to shop for and prepare our food each day.

My favorite dish is spaghetti and meat sauce; the house smells so good when I come home, that my mouth begins to water. If she's in a good mood, Mother will even allow me to taste a tablespoon of the sauce before it's done cooking. I could eat her spaghetti every night. But we must also eat yukky liver and onions because my parents think that it's good for us. We love it when Daddy gets home from work a bit earlier than usual because he cooks some bacon to add to the liver. This way Paul and I can manage to swallow it.

Tonight, Mother has made split pea soup—another one of my favorites. It's so warm and smooth, and it makes me feel so good inside. We always have a chopped green salad with our dinner. And, of course, milk. Every morning, the milkman delivers four glass quarts of milk to the aluminum case that sits on our back porch. Mother has made it very clear that each day, we are expected to drink a quart of milk.

A few times a year, Mother makes something called Brown Betty—a mixture of apple slices, cinnamon, and brown sugar. Since we hardly ever get to eat anything that's sweet, this is a big treat. Tonight, as usual, there's nothing sweet to eat after dinner. But Mother reminds us to have one more glass of milk before we go to our bedroom.

January 1964

On weekends, I miss going to school, but I'm glad I get to see Daddy more often. This afternoon the four of us will go to A&P Supermarket like we always do on Saturdays. I like going to the supermarket because I get to see so many different types of food—most that we never have in our house. I love all the colors and happy sounds of the supermarket, too. I watch the people and try to imagine where they live. I wonder if any of them live close to me.

"Paul, Christine—get in the car! We're ready to go!"

Paul and I close the books that we've been reading in our beds and hurry to follow Daddy and Mother out the front door. We begin the drive to the A&P that's not too far from our home.

When we arrive, we get out of the car and follow Daddy and Mother inside. They always buy the fruits and vegetables first, and as they make their way there, I see a large display of boxes at the end of the aisle. Two beautiful blond-haired dolls are out of their boxes and are sitting at school desks. Behind each of them is a blackboard. Each box says in big red letters, Suzy Smart, and has a picture of the doll holding up her hand in a school classroom. I read the words that are printed on three other blackboards on the box that say, "I can talk! I can spell! I can add!" I can't stop looking at Suzy. I feel like I'm in the classroom with her right now.

After a few moments, I look for Daddy and Mother and see them down the aisle putting some broccoli into a plastic bag.

"Come here, Christine," I hear Daddy say.

But I don't want to leave Suzy. She's wearing a red plaid dress, and there's a small black hat on her blond hair. Her blue eyes look like they can even open and close! She is so beautiful.

I run down the aisle to Daddy and Mother.

"I just saw a doll named Suzy Smart! Can you please buy her for me? Please? I don't have any dolls to play with at home, and she even talks! I promise I'll take care of her."

"I'm sorry, Christine, but right now we don't have money for things like that," Daddy says.

"Let me see the doll, Christine," I hear my mother say.

I walk with Mother back to the display, and she looks at Suzy Smart. Then she lifts her up out of her desk and presses down right in the middle of her chest. Suzy starts to speak!

"Hi, my name is Suzy Smart. What's your name? I can spell. Cat—C-A-T. Dog—D-O-G. I can do arithmetic. 2+2=4. 4+4=8. I can recite. Twinkle, twinkle, little star. How I wonder what you are."

I look at Mother. She seems interested in Suzy, too, as she is now touching her red dress, the blackboard, and her black shoes.

A few minutes later I hear her say, "I think we need to buy this for Christine, Charlie. This is not just a normal doll but a smart doll. We can afford it."

"Thank you, thank you!" I give Mother a great big hug.

I pick up an unopened box and put it into their cart. I can't wait to get home and take Suzy Smart out of her box. Now, even when I'm not at school, I can still be in a school at my house and have Suzy as my friend.

May 1964

We load into the blue Chevrolet Biscayne. It's moving day. A chance for a fresh start. Paul is now ten, and I'm almost seven. We sit in the backseat as Daddy drives us to our new home. Daddy told us that it is a split-level model house at 97 Rumford Road—only eight miles away from Commack in a city called Kings Park.

Things between my mother and Mr. Grogan had gotten worse and worse. It seemed like Mother was just waiting for him to leave his house, so she could yell at him some more. I had seen him talk to Daddy many times, and I could tell by the look on his face that he was always very angry. Daddy said that Mr. Grogan was threatening us, so we had to do something about it. I didn't want to leave our home at 3 Rockland Court, but Daddy told me and Paul that this move will be an opportunity for our mother to leave all her "nonsense" behind in our old house.

As we are driving to Kings Park, Daddy turns to Mother and says, "We are starting a new life, Sophie. You are going to leave all this witchcraft behind; do you hear me?" Silence. His voice begins to rise. "I have worked very hard so we can afford to move to our new house, and this witchcraft is staying in Commack. You are going to behave yourself. Do you hear me?"

Paul and I sit in silence as we watch our mother half-listen to him. It's still so clear that she is sick. We watch as her left index finger moves in and out from her nose. She has told us that when she does this, she is "stopping the curse" she feels and is cursing back whomever she thinks is cursing her.

Daddy keeps driving and is getting more and more angry with each mile. Mother's motions continue. Suddenly, he takes his hand off the steering wheel and strikes her arm trying to keep her from continuing her motions.

A screaming match begins, as does a new chapter of my family's life.

October 1964

I think Daddy thinks that I'm spending too much time by myself. Because of his job as a clerk at the court, by the time he gets home from Brooklyn, it's sometimes after seven o'clock.

One Saturday he tells me he has a surprise for me waiting in the car. I walk out to the car and look into the backseat window. Through it, I see the cutest dog I've ever seen. He is small and has a white coat with a few light brown markings. His thin tail is wagging so much.

Mother has heard us talking and walks down the driveway to join us at the car. She looks into the backseat window to see the dog and then tells us that God has just told her what the dog's name will be—Wisdom. *Wisdom?* Who has ever named a dog Wisdom? Clearly, someone without much of it.

I reach in to pick up Wisdom and let him out of the car. I place him on the ground and call for him to follow me, and he does—right up the walkway stairs and into our house. For the next few hours I feel the happiest I've been in a long time. Wisdom follows me everywhere—to the backyard, to my bedroom, and even to the bathroom. Somehow, he knows that he's my dog.

That weekend, Paul and I train him to wee and poop outside. Then in our backyard, we throw tennis balls for him to fetch, and he runs all over scooping them up. He can't bring them back to us yet, but it's so much fun to see him run after them. We finally are away from the darkness that is inside our house.

On Sunday, Paul and I decide to call Wisdom "Wissie" for short, as the name suits him much better—Mother can keep calling him Wisdom if she wants to. We begin to teach Wissie to walk on a leash. Finally, something has pulled Paul out of his bedroom where he usually spends most of his free time reading. It's so much fun to get out of the house together and walk our dog.

On Monday, I know I must leave Wissie and go to school. Tears quickly fill my eyes when I think of leaving him—especially leaving him with my mother. I can't imagine her caring for him and playing with him. What will she do with him all day? What if she begins to think that Wissie is also a demon?

The bell to end another day of second grade can't come quickly enough. I rush to get my notebooks, and then I walk as fast as I can to get home. As I walk into the house, I expect Wissie to be at the front door waiting for me, but I don't see him anywhere. I rush through the house and open the back door to look for him in our backyard. He isn't there either. I start to panic. Where can he be?

I call out to my mother, "Mother? Mother? Where is Wissie?"

I hear her voice from the back bedroom. "He was digging up our garden, so I took him back to the shelter."

December 1964

I still miss Wissie, and I plead with Daddy to get me another dog. He tells me that dogs are destructive and take lots of work, but he'll consider getting me a cat.

This time he asks me to join him on the trip to the animal shelter. We drive to the Northport Animal Shelter, and I excitedly walk in and quickly see so many beautiful cats that could be adopted. After slowly looking at each one, I ask the attendant if I can pick up the only cat there that has white fur. She purrs as soon as I pick her up, so I know she is the one. I name her Twinkle.

What a difference Twinkle quickly makes in my life! I get to come home to her every day, and this time my daddy has told Mother that she needs to keep her hands off her. Even though she's still quite young, Twinkle must remain an outside cat, though, as my mother tells us that she doesn't want Twinkle's hair all over our house. Since our house is constantly a mess and smells nasty, I can't imagine why a little cat hair bothers her.

Before long, Twinkle seems to be getting fatter, and Daddy tells me he thinks she's pregnant. For the next few months, Daddy, Paul, and I watch her closely as she prepares to become a mom.

One cold Sunday morning, Twinkle chooses to give birth to her litter of kittens under my bed. Even with the newspapers that Daddy has put there to keep my floor from getting dirty, there is still lots of blood and goop everywhere.

I don't care because four tiny baby kittens have been born! I hear them making tiny sounds, and they don't even have their eyes open yet. It looks like two of them are white like Twinkle, but the others have grey spots on their tiny bodies. I name them Cutie, Whitey, Snowball, and Snowflake.

Twinkle spends the next few days under my bed as she cares for her babies. I guess she knows that it's the safest place in our house. After a week, the kittens slowly begin to open their eyes. I spend many hours each day watching them as Twinkle lets them suck on her to get milk and then licks them over and over so they will be clean. Twinkle is such a kind and loving mom. I wish I had a mother like her.

April 1965

Once we moved away from Larry Grogan on Rockland Court, we hoped that Mother wouldn't find any other neighbors she considered to be demonic in our new neighborhood on Rumford Road. But as it turns out, it only gets worse. It doesn't take long for our new neighbors to find out how strange we are. I'm sure it seems like two grandparents are raising their grandchildren, a boy who looks to be around twelve whom they rarely see, and me, a girl of around eight who often sits alone in front of her house holding a white cat.

My mother's satanic world has grown. Now she thinks that every person she meets is putting a curse on her by his or her actions, and it is her God-given job to stop the curse and then curse the person back. She thinks that people curse her through the colors of the clothes they wear—black, red, and purple being the worst—and if they happen to touch any area of their bodies when they talk to her. Then it becomes her job to curse them back through her hand movements—back and forth from her nose, or from her forehead to the back of her gray hair.

The most disgusting thing happens when she sometimes even spreads her legs and pees on the ground in order to curse them back. She calls her urine her "holy water." One conversation with my Mother is all that any of our neighbors need to know that she is a crazy woman. No wonder we're left alone and never get to know any of them.

After a year of living at this house, my mother decides that she must have a white marble house with purple shutters to live in, as that's the type of house that God has told her our house should be. How she convinces Daddy to agree to have the front of our house marbled, I'll never understand. He has always been the only one who earns money in our family. Once he even told me how thankful he is for his friend Walter Lord, a lawyer he works with, as Daddy sometimes gets a twenty-dollar loan from him just to get our family through the month.

But he gives in to Mother's strange wish, and before you know it, not only does a crazy woman live in our house, but our house also looks different from every other house in the neighborhood.

September 1965

I just finished another day in third grade with Mrs. Cotter. As soon as I open the door to my house, Mother tells me to come to the kitchen. Like she had done before, she tells me I have to drink this nasty drink she's making for me. I don't want to because not only do I see a raw egg floating in it, but I also see a strange dark brown powder on top of the egg and milk that she is getting ready to whip in the blender.

"No, I'm not going to drink it! And nothing you do will make me!"

"You are just like the rest of them. Get out of my house, you little demon!"

I can't wait to.

I walk outside the front door, quickly run down the steps, lift the white garage door, and find my blue bicycle. I'm going to ride as far away from my mother as I can get. I move my bike down the driveway and push off. The next thing I hear is the screech of a car. I hear someone scream, "Oh, my God!"

I feel myself being thrown into the air, and I land face down on the concrete. I begin to cry out in pain. The next thing I see are two people I don't know. I see a man looking down on me, and I hear a woman say, "I bet she lives there. Let me go see if her mom or dad is home."

I can't move my legs at all. I turn my face to the side and taste something strange. Then I see blood on the pavement where my face had been resting. I start crying louder and can't stop.

I hear my Mother's voice in the distance scream out, "What did you demons do to my daughter? We must get her to a doctor right away!"

I feel many hands picking me up, but I'm still lying down. I've never felt so much pain. It hurts so much to move. Then everything goes black.

I wake up in a doctor's office, and when I open my eyes, I see a woman with a white hat looking down at me. I hear the voice of a man say, "Don't worry, honey. You will be okay. I need to examine you and see where all your bruises are. You are such a brave girl. We will clean you up, and you'll be okay, I promise."

Everything is black again.

When I wake up, I hear a voice that sounds like my daddy's voice. I slowly open my eyes and see his face close to mine. His body is bent, and it looks like he is kneeling on the floor. I hear him say, "Thank you, God. Thank you for letting this not be more serious than it could have been. Thanks for protecting my Christine."

His voice seems to break. I look closer and see tears on his cheeks. I've never seen my daddy cry before.

January 1966

After all the threats Daddy has told us our neighbors have made about his need to control Mother's behavior, it has finally happened: I walk home from school and discover that my mother is gone. I know Paul won't be arriving home from school for an hour, so I sit in my bedroom stroking Twinkle and waiting for Paul to return. Where could Mother be? I check and see that our car is still in the garage, so she hasn't driven anywhere.

A few minutes later, a taxi pulls up in front of our house, and Daddy gets out. What is he doing home from work so early? He walks inside our home, gives me a hug, and asks if I'm all right.

"I'm fine, but where's Mother?"

"Our neighbors finally had enough of Mother's demonic antics. They called the cops on her this morning, and right now she's at the Kings Park State Hospital being evaluated. I'm so glad that she had her mental faculties enough to tell them where I worked. When I got the call, I left right away. I'm so glad you're okay, Christine."

We learn that night that Mother will be committed to the mental hospital and will begin to get the medicine she needs to take all her sickness away. We'll be able to visit her in a week. For the first time in a very long time, I'm not holding my breath.

May 1966

Mother has been back from the hospital for a month now. When she first came home, she was very weak and just lay upstairs on the couch all day and night. But slowly her energy has come back, and from her behavior, I can tell that she'll soon be getting sick again.

The signs are all there: She's started to talk about demons and witches again. She's started to make her cursing-them-back movements. She eats constantly, even foods with lots of sugar that she tells us not to eat because they are bad for us. She sleeps very little because she stays up for most of each night cursing all the demons she feels are out there trying to get her.

When I return from school one afternoon and walk into our kitchen to get an afternoon snack, I decide to make some milk out of Alba powdered milk. I reach inside the Alba box and see half a bar of Hershey's milk chocolate. Mother is outside watering the front lawn, so I know that I should move quickly. I grab the chocolate bar and leave the kitchen, heading for my bedroom. Sitting on my bed, I open the wrapping carefully as I know this is a rare and unexpected treasure. I must eat it before my mother finds out I took it.

If heaven has a taste, this is it. I tear off each square piece-by-piece, and as each one melts in my mouth, I feel like I am transported to another place; quickly, I feel so much happier.

But now I hear her yelling at someone. Her sharp voice comes through the window.

"I don't need to be dealing with you! Get off my property right now! You are a bastard and a wizard!"

I get up and look through the window just in time to see my mother lift up her nylon dress and expose her naked body to our next-door neighbor. I watch as he quickly goes back inside his house. I breathe a sigh of relief.

A few minutes later, I hear sirens in the distance, and then a police car stops in front of our house. I watch as two policemen get out and approach my mother. I stand at the window, barely moving the drapes out of the way so I can see what's happening. I don't want them to know that I'm there.

I hear Mother arguing with them about something, but I can't completely understand what she's saying. Then I see one of the officers take out a pair of handcuffs and put them around my mother's wrists. Her screaming grows louder as I hear her cursing at the officers at the top of her lungs.

Once they have my mother in handcuffs, the policemen put her in the back seat of their car. Thankfully, she must not have said anything about me being inside because the police car starts up and heads down the street.

An hour later Paul returns from school, and I tell him what happened. Together, we wait for Daddy to come home. We have no idea where our mother is, but that doesn't matter. Thankfully, she is out of the house again.

June 1966

Yesterday was the last day of school. It is Saturday, and Daddy is taking me to the Kings Park Library. I love going to the library with him because I get to check out as many books as I want. When I read them, I feel like I'm far away from my house and my mother.

When we arrive, a nice lady asks me if I want to join the Summer Reading Program.

"What is that?" I ask.

She tells me that they'll keep track of all the books I'll read during the summer. When I return the books, I'll get to choose one sticker for each book that I read. I'll get to fill up my own poster that will hang in the library. It will have my name on it, and at the end of the summer there will be a grand prize for the person who reads the most books.

"Do you want to join the program?"

"Yes!" I tell her.

I fill out my name, address, and phone number on a small piece of white paper, and she shows me the empty poster that I can begin to fill up with stickers as soon as I return the first books. Unfortunately, during the summer I can only check out four books at a time.

I spend time looking for books that I know I'll read. *The Pink Dress* is one of them. So is *A Wrinkle in Time* and *Anne of Green Gables.*

After I've found four books, I make my way up to the circulation desk, and the lady checks them out.

Daddy and I walk out of the library and head back home. I can't wait to start reading and fill my poster in with the cool-looking stickers. Maybe I can even win the grand prize!

A few months later, I'm so happy when I find out that I did read more books than anyone else that summer, and I won the grand prize—a bright blue leather book bag to carry all my books.

July 1967

It's a sunny morning, and I'm seated in our car with my daddy and Paul. We're on the way to one of my favorite places for the day, Sunken Meadow State Park. My stomach hurts. I've only eaten a banana for breakfast, so I don't know why it is hurting. It just feels strange.

In only ten minutes, we arrive at the beach, and my pain doesn't go away, even when I start swimming in the cold, salty water.

After a couple of hours of swimming and sunning on our large blanket, we head back up to the boardwalk for our usual lunch: hamburgers, milk, and if Daddy can be persuaded, a box of Cracker Jacks or a soft vanilla ice cream cone. I'm not that hungry today, though, because my stomach is still hurting. Daddy asks me why I haven't finished my hamburger, and I tell him that I'm not very hungry. This is a first, because the saltwater and sunshine always make me extremely hungry.

Before we go back down to the beach, I head to the women's restroom. When I pull down the bottom of my two-piece bathing suit, I'm horrified to see a dark stain on the panty lining.

Oh, my God! What is that? Am I going to die?

Then I remember that just last week in our science class, the girls had gone into a special room to watch a film about something that will be happening to us in two or three more years; we will start to menstruate. Could this dark stain be blood? Even though I've learned that most girls start to menstruate at around twelve years old, could I be starting to menstruate two years earlier?

I grab a large wad of toilet paper and clean myself off; as I do, I notice that more blood has come from between my legs. I grab another wad of toilet paper and make a ball and put it in the place between my legs where the blood may be coming from. Then I pull up my swimsuit bottom, wash my hands, and walk back outside into the bright sun.

What should I do now? What if it isn't blood but something more serious? My heart is pounding. I sure can't talk to my daddy or to Paul about this! But how can I tell my sick mother about it? How will she react?

Daddy sees me coming. "Are you okay, Christine?"

I shake my head. "I really don't feel very good right now. My tummy hurts a lot. Can we go home?"

"Yes. I'm so sorry that you aren't feeling well. When we get home, I want you to just rest, okay?"

I nod.

On the way home, Daddy and Paul talk in the front seat while I sit quietly in the back seat, getting more and more scared the closer we get to my house.

By the time we pull into the driveway, I know that I have no other choice: I must find my mother and tell her about this. What if something else is wrong with me? My stomach is still hurting, so maybe there is.

We enter the house, and I suspect my mother is either in the bathtub, where she often stays for hours on end, or upstairs, lying on her couch that stinks from her urine. I find her in the bathtub.

"Can I come in?" I ask at the bathroom door. "I have something important to tell you."

"Come in, Christine," she responds in her shrill voice.

I enter and try not to look at her ugly body lying in a foot of water. Her large, sloppy breasts are lying on her big, white stomach. I see the pink outline of her c-section scar—the one that I was born from—and my stomach pain intensifies. A few hairs from her private parts float in the water.

I tell her that I haven't felt well today as my stomach has been hurting, and I think that I may need to see a doctor. She looks up and suddenly seems very concerned.

"What's wrong?" she asks.

I take a deep breath.

"When we were at the beach today, I had to go to the bathroom. When I pulled down my bathing suit bottom, there was a dark red stain on it. I don't know if I should go to a doctor."

My mother sits up more quickly than I have ever seen her move before.

"Yes, we will definitely be going to a doctor." By the frightened look on her face, I'm beginning to think that her fear may not be about my having started to menstruate.

My mother has not driven for a long time, but somehow, she convinces my daddy that she needs to drive me by herself to the doctor. The entire way there, she is more serious and focused than I've ever seen her.

We arrive at the same doctor's office that I had been taken to when I was hit by a car on my bike; thankfully, it's only a few miles away. My mother quickly walks up to the registration desk and tells the receptionist that we must see a doctor because something terrible has happened to her daughter.

Something terrible? Is starting to menstruate something terrible?

Because we don't have an appointment, it seems like hours before we are called back to see the doctor, a kind-looking, middle-aged man. How I wish I could talk to a lady doctor about this! My mother tells him about her concern that something terrible could have happened to me. Was I taken advantage of? I don't have any idea what she could be talking about.

Then a blonde-headed nurse walks into our room, and I breathe a sigh of relief. She's very nice to me as she tells me that I need to take off all my clothes, to cover myself with the white sheet, and then she and the doctor will examine me. She asks my mother to leave the room; they'll let her know how I am as soon as they finish examining me.

"Christine, I need to ask you what may be a very difficult question for you to answer. Have any boys or men seen your private parts recently?"

"Of course not!"

"Great. Thanks for letting us know."

The doctor asks me to open my legs. I have never shown this part of my body to anyone, and I'm shaking so hard. But I know I must obey.

He examines my private girl-part while the nurse holds my hand and keeps repeating, "Everything is going to be okay, honey. Everything is going to be okay."

His gloved fingers hurt me as they poke up inside my body—I think the movie we'd seen had a name for that part of my body, but I can't remember what it's called. He slowly pulls his fingers out and then asks me if I've been feeling any pain today. I tell him that I've felt stomach pain all day—but the pain is in my lower stomach. After examining the other parts of me, he tells me that I am a brave girl and that I'll be fine—nothing is wrong with me. Before he leaves the room, he tells me that the nurse will explain everything to me.

"Christine, you have begun to menstruate—something that all young women do. The pain that you've been feeling is the normal cramping that many girls experience at this time of the month. The pain should go away in a few days. Now that you are a young woman, you are going to need to learn how to use this, too."

She shows me a long, padded napkin and an elastic belt that I can attach the napkin to and tells me to slip it on—it will hold all the blood that will still come out for a few more days. I had seen long napkins like this in a drawer in my mother's bureau and didn't know what they were for. I feel so uncomfortable because I sure don't want to share this part of being a woman with my mother.

When we get back to our car, my mother seems relieved. She tells me that since I am a young menstruating woman now, I can get pregnant if I let any man's private parts get close to mine. Then she lowers her head, moves her face close to mine, looks right into my eyes, and in a serious voice says, "Men are going to want to do this to you, so you need to make sure it doesn't ever happen."

I nod.

A couple of years ago, Paul had told me how a girl gets pregnant. Now it all is beginning to make sense. But all I want to do is to get back home to my bedroom, lie down in my bed, suck my thumb, flick my finger on my pillowcase, and cry.

September 1967

We have lived in the model house for three years. I love my bright bedroom at the front of the house. It has a big window that's covered with light yellow curtains that let lots of sunshine in. Since my parents bought a model house, it also came with all the furniture it needed and lots of other things, like even the vases on the coffee tables and many pictures on the walls.

My room has become my happy place. Now I realize I have total control to keep my room organized and clean; this way, at least one room in the house will look like the houses of my friends Beverly and Regina. I glance over at my wicker chair and see a huge pile of clothes on it—clothes that I have put there because I don't want to take the time to hang them up. I decide that if I want my room to look good, I must hang up all the clothes I wear and never leave anything lying on the floor anymore. Everything has a place, and all I need to do is to put each thing back in its place. No matter how out-of-control my mother is, I'll now have total control over my neat and organized room. This feels so comforting.

But today I've come home from school, and I can't get away from her. She follows me from room to room in the house, up the stairs to the playroom, and then down again and through the back hall to my bedroom. As she follows me, her index finger moves in and out from her nose. Once again, she thinks that I've cursed her in some way, and she's cursing me back to take the curse away.

The only room in our house with a lock on the door is the bathroom. I open it and quickly shut her out, locking the door behind me. I sit down on the toilet seat and breathe in a few breaths of relief. She can't follow me in here.

After a few moments, I glance up at the purple tile on my right. I see the squares once again—each one so precise, so perfect, the grout snuggled inside, filling up each crack. I close my fist and begin to rap on the tiles, hoping that with each rap, she will magically appear to comfort me.

Tap, Tap, Tap. Three across.

Tap, Tap, Tap. Three underneath.

Clap. Clap. Clap.

Nothing.

"Jeannie?" I say out loud. "Jeannie?"

Finally, I get a response.

Hello, Christine. I'm here for you. It's going to be okay.

I breathe a sigh of relief. I am once again with my special friend. I'm not alone anymore with my wild animal of a mother. Jeannie sees my mother, but unlike when others see her, I don't have to run away embarrassed and hope that nobody will find out that ten years ago I was cut out of this woman's body.

November 1967

When I return home from school each day, no matter what condition I find my mother in, I know that in just a few hours, thankfully, Daddy will be home. Most days I enter the smelly house and find her still sitting on the couch where I had left her that morning—still lost in her world of "cursing the devil."

It took some convincing, but Daddy finally bought a 12" black-and-white TV that he keeps on the floor in the corner of his bedroom—a TV "just to be used on special occasions"—like to watch the Billy Graham crusades, *The Lawrence Welk Show*, and the Olympics. I've been told that I'm not supposed to watch TV because of "all the garbage on the worldly shows," but I quickly learn that all I have to do is to lift the TV to the top of my mother's bureau and plug it in, and my daddy will never know that I have watched it—as long as it is back in its place before he returns home from work.

Finally, I have something to look forward to after school—something to take my mind off the reality of what I'm coming home to. I head back to my parents' bedroom and tightly close the door to their room. I quietly pick up the TV and turn on whatever is on that I can escape to. The after-school shows are *The Munsters*, *Bewitched*, and *Dark Shadows*. I keep the volume turned down so Mother won't hear what I'm doing. Each show is about a person who has unusual powers in some way—and right outside the bedroom door, I live with a woman called my mother who also has unusual powers.

December 1967

Mother is the worst I've ever seen her, and I'm never happy at home—even after my daddy returns home from work late each afternoon. He has all he can do to control her. She's been hospitalized so many times, but nothing has worked to keep her well; after just a few months at home, she always returns to her demons and crazy behavior. And by this time, my daddy has also learned that the only way he can get her to a mental hospital, anyway, is if the police come and put her into a straitjacket. For this to happen, she must make a major disturbance—usually one where she yells nasty things at people, lifts her nylon dress and shows them her private parts, and then sometimes urinates on the ground.

Most of the time I remain in my bedroom holding my feather pillow to my head and sucking on my left thumb, which is already quite flat from the hours that I suck on it each day. Unlike my other friends, I have very few toys to play with. Without my summer library books, the only things in our house to read are copies of *The Holy Bible, Reader's Digest*, and *Moody Monthly*, a Christian magazine. And of course, nobody can ever see how crazy my mother is, so I can never have any of my school friends over to my house.

I'm in the fifth grade at Park View Elementary School, a neighborhood school about half a mile from our home. It's December, and cold winter weather has come to Kings Park.

One afternoon, I'm sitting at my desk listening to Mr. Dinora teach us about the planets. Suddenly, the classroom door swings wide open. I can't believe it—my disgusting mother has just walked into the classroom! She storms up to Mr. Dinora, who is clearly unsure of who this person is and what to do about it.

At the top of her voice my mother yells, "Mr. Dinora, you son-of-a-bitch! You are a wizard and a demon, and the FBI is after you!"

Then she turns to me, and in a high-pitched voice exclaims, "Come on home, Christine. You don't need to be in this school anymore. You are a virgin Jew like me. Come on home."

I sit there paralyzed. I begin to shake all over. Mr. Dinora's face has turned a bright red, and he is silent. When my mother sees that I won't move, she turns away and walks out of the classroom.

I sit there shocked and embarrassed. My secret is out. Now, no matter how nice I am to the other kids in my class, they will know that this fat, disgusting woman is my mother.

I'll always be known as "the crazy woman's daughter."

February 1968

Most of my friends are happy when it's Friday. But I hate Fridays because I know that in two days it will be Sunday, the day that our family goes to church. Already we have gone through four churches. As soon as Mother gets too comfortable in any church, she begins to talk to the people sitting near us and tells them all the things the Bible says about witchcraft. I often hear her recite her favorite verse in the Old Testament: "Thou shalt not suffer a witch to live." Once she talks to somebody, I never see them again. I think they are still at the church but are sitting in pews very far from our pew.

Three years ago, Paul and I were baptized in Plainview Baptist Church, a church that I really liked. But then one Sunday morning right in the middle of the sermon, Mother stood up and started spouting out crazy words about witchcraft. I sat there frozen, so embarrassed and unable to do anything about it.

As soon as she sat down, Daddy yanked on her arm and said, "Okay, Sophie. That is enough. Let's go." He pulled her out of her seat and escorted her down the main aisle and out of the church. Paul and I followed along behind them. I kept my head turned down, too embarrassed to look at anyone. We never returned to that church.

Today, we are visiting Commack Baptist Church. I don't want to go, but with both my mother and Daddy insisting that we try another church, and Mother telling Daddy that she will behave this time, I know I have no choice but to join them.

An hour later I slowly follow my parents into the sanctuary. I sit down in the pew, begin to color on the children's bulletin, and start to pray. "God, please keep my mother's mouth closed this morning. Please."

April 1968

I must escape from her nasty smell and her awful actions. Quickly, the front porch and front yard become my refuge. I crave something sweet to eat, but as always, because my mother and Daddy only want me to eat healthy food, there is nothing sweet in our house other than a jar with honey and a jar with molasses.

I get a wax paper bag and open the cabinet where we keep our vitamins. My mother and Daddy always make sure that I take many of them every day. The ones that I can chew are the sour vitamin C tablets and the brewer's yeast tablets that have a slightly sweet taste to them. I fill up the small wax paper bag with brewer's yeast tablets.

I walk outside and down the concrete path and take a seat on one of the steps. I look out to the many houses around me and start mindlessly, one by one, putting each tablet into my mouth. I chew each one hard, tasting a bit of sweetness. I feel the strong smell and taste. For a few minutes, I am numb to what is going on behind the front door of my house. Over and over, my hand keeps moving to my mouth.

May 1968

It's bedtime, my favorite part of each day as I know that for just a few minutes, I'll have Daddy all to myself. "Daddy, I'm ready!"

He enters my bedroom with a smile on his face and tells me to scoot over as he sits down on the side of my bed. First, it is time to get my back rubbed. I slowly turn over, and he begins to rub my back. I feel my body relax as soon as his strong, loving hands begin to slowly move over my back. From my back he moves to my neck, shoulders, and then finally, he rubs each of my arms. He tells me to lift my head, and then he removes my feather pillow and fluffs it up so that it will be softer for me.

Finally, he reaches for my hand and begins to pray. Most of the time, I don't listen to the words he says too closely—it's just his soothing voice that puts me to sleep.

Tonight, I hear him begin, "God, thank you for this day that you have given us. We know that no matter how hard things are, that You are with us. Please help Mother to get rid of the demonic spirit that has overtaken her life..."

June 1968

I've just finished sixth grade, so my time at Park View Elementary School has finally come to an end. A tall man with black-rimmed glasses named Mr. Cronin was my teacher this year. I was so scared when I saw his name on the letter that was sent home at the end of last summer because some of my friends had told me how mean he was, but he ended up being the best teacher I've ever had. He explained things really well, and he made learning so much fun—especially with the impersonations of people he often did.

Since kindergarten, I've loved going to school, and each year I thought that I might want to be a teacher someday; this year I had so much fun in Mr. Cronin's class that I decided that I definitely want to be a teacher when I grow up.

The first weekend of summer, my mother announces that we will be visiting my Uncle Nat and Aunt Rea that weekend. I couldn't have heard better news. My mother's brother is one of my favorite people in the world. Next to my daddy, when I'm with Uncle Nat, I always feel the most loved.

Early on Saturday morning, Paul and I slide into the backseat of our bright blue Chevrolet Biscayne, and my daddy begins the two-and-a-half-hour drive to Asbury Park.

For as long as I can remember, we have been visiting my Uncle Nat twice a year. When I was five, Uncle Nat married a beautiful woman named Rea. Ever since their unforgettable wedding in Philadelphia, I now also have an aunt to visit whenever we visit him. But Uncle Nat always is still the main attraction.

Unlike my mother, he can't stop smiling about everything and is so much fun to be around. He always takes me and Paul to places that our parents never would take us, like to amusement parks, and he buys us foods that we never are allowed to eat, like cotton candy. My mother hates how much of "the world" he gives us, but when she protests, he always says, "Sophie, they are children, and they need to do things that children do."

The only time I see Uncle Nat angry is when my mother endlessly keeps trying to convert him from Judaism to Christianity telling him that he will be damned to hell because he has not accepted Jesus Christ as his personal Savior. From what I can see, it looks like if anyone will be damned to hell, it will be my mother, not Uncle Nat.

Like always, this trip turns out to be so much fun. We spend hours together walking on the beautiful Asbury Park boardwalk, and we stop to eat at a restaurant that my parents would never go to because it is too expensive.

When we walk back to our car to say goodbye, Uncle Nat takes my hand and tells me to stop walking for a moment because he has something to give me. He puts his hand into his coat jacket and takes out a small square box.

"This is a radio," he says. "You need to start listening to music that kids your age are listening to, not just to the music your mom and dad listen to."

I take it from him and give him a big hug. It is the coolest-looking gift I have ever received. When we return to our house, it doesn't take me long to find WABC. In the solitude of my bedroom, I start listening to rock'n'roll music that I had always been told I shouldn't listen to. I hear "Hey, Jude," "Mrs. Robinson," and "The Green Tambourine." Quickly, I am transported to another world as I feel every beat, memorize every word, and finally feel connected to the outside world.

October 1968

Her urine smell and stains are everywhere—on the sheets to her bed, on the sofa where she sits, on the throw pillows she leans against, and on every carpet throughout our house. Due to a call made to the police by one of our neighbors, my mother is in the state mental hospital again. But still, nothing we do can get her putrid smell out.

Daddy tries apple cider vinegar, but it doesn't work. Clorox cleaner doesn't help either. I want so much to forget about her and to pretend that she doesn't exist. With her gone, I don't ever worry about what I will come home to at the end of my school days. With her gone, I don't have to be afraid of what she will say or do on Sunday mornings when we attend church. With her gone, it's just me, Paul, and my daddy living in peace. She can't come back home.

Please, Daddy. Please don't let her ever come home again.

But after a couple of months, she is better, and my daddy says she must come home "where she belongs."

Once again, she comes home and is very quiet. She walks around our house like a zombie; clearly, she is still drugged. She says she's very tired, and she spends most of each day in the bathtub for hours or lying on the sofa upstairs. But for now, she is not out of control. My daddy tells me not to drink the milk because he has put her medication in it. He knows she won't take her medication any other way. If she can drink enough milk, she shouldn't ever be sick again.

But after just a few weeks at home, she begins to live in her imaginary world again where we are all witches and wizards, and her God-given job is to cast these demons out.

December 1968

The medicine in the milk sure doesn't help Mother; in less than two months, once again, she thinks that each of us is cursing her. Because it has been snowing and is so cold outside, my daddy knows that with my mother's satanic antics, it will be a long weekend for the three of us to be cooped up in the house with her. We must get out. Paul decides he wants to stay reading, so it will just be the two of us.

I love to get in the car with Daddy and go for a car ride. Sometimes we just drive around King's Park, and other times we drive farther out on the island. Often, we go to the nearby boardwalk at Sunken Meadow State Park and walk together, always holding hands. I feel so safe and loved when I'm with him.

One of the other best parts of going for a drive with him is that he usually stops somewhere to get some food that I know my mother would never allow in the house. If we're at the beach, he buys me a box of Cracker Jacks that even has a little toy inside. If we're hungry, on the way home, he'll stop and buy each of us a slice of yummy pizza at Pizza D'More. And if it's summer, he will stop at Carvel ice cream shop where I order a vanilla/chocolate swirl ice cream cone—my favorite treat in the world.

This afternoon, because it's too cold to go to the beach, we stop for a slice of pizza. Rather than take it with us like we usually do, this time he tells me to sit down with him at a small table. He has something that he wants to tell me.

"I know how hard it is for you when Mother is sick, Christine. But I also know that we both need to keep praying for her to get well. God hears our prayers, and He'll answer them if we just keep praying. It may not be right away that He answers them, but if we keep praying and have faith, it is going to happen."

Somehow, I believe him.

January 1969

"Now I Belong to Jesus"

Jesus, my Lord will love me forever,
From Him no power of evil can sever,
He gave His life to ransom my soul, Now I belong to Him.
Now I belong to Jesus, Jesus belongs to me,
Not for the years of time alone, But for eternity.
Once I was lost in sin's degradation,
Jesus came down to bring me salvation,
Lifted me up from sorrow and shame, Now I belong to Him.
Now I belong to Jesus, Jesus belongs to me,
Not for the years of time alone, But for eternity.
Joy floods my soul, for Jesus has saved me,
Freed me from sin that long had enslaved me,
His precious blood He gave to redeem, Now I belong to Him.
Now I belong to Jesus, Jesus belongs to me,
Not for the years of time alone, But for eternity.

By the time I'm eleven, I know every word of this hymn, backwards and forwards. My mother has played it on the small portable organ in our den hundreds of times. She sings it in the morning before I go to school, in the afternoons when I return, and whenever the mood strikes her in the evenings. Like her speaking voice, her singing voice is shrill, and as she sings, she plays the melody in her right hand—her left hand hits random keys. I don't know who taught her to read music, but somehow, she reads just enough to get the tune out…over and over.

How I wish she did belong to Jesus. And how I wish that right now, she would take her stinking smell and hateful mouth and crazy hands and disgusting urine out of our house.

For eternity.

February 1969

Unlike the other artwork that came with our model house, I can't stop looking at the picture in our front hallway of a young Amish woman. She is wearing a simple navy-blue dress and a white apron and bonnet, and she is sitting alone in her chair, peeling potatoes. The expression on her face is so sad. I often find myself gazing up at her, wishing that I could be there with her so she would have a friend. And she could be mine.

Today when I come home from school, I walk in and find a urine-filled house gone mad. There are blood stains all over the walls in the front hallway, and all the artwork in the house is off the walls. The Amish woman is gone.

I find my mother in the back hallway with a kitchen knife in her hand. Blood is dripping down her arm, but I don't care.

"Where is the painting of the woman peeling potatoes?"

"Look outside," she responds. "She is a demon, so I had to get her out of our house."

I open the front door, and rain is coming down in sheets. I quickly look all over the front lawn and finally see her. She is leaning against the fence to my right, but it's too late. The rain has already damaged her beyond repair. Once again, because of the hateful work of my mother, in just a few moments, another friend of mine is gone.

April 1969
Age 11

As I sit in this crowded, noisy classroom
I am lost.
The crowd discourages
The noise aggravates
The color blinds
I am lost.
The people seek but don't find
The girls try but don't succeed
But one does
I am lost.
The only one who succeeds is a
proud longhaired beautiful tramp
(you know the type)
They all follow this thing
but I don't
I'm still lost.
Maybe someday I'll find
what I'm looking for.

June 1969

I'm so happy that seventh grade is over. It was hard to move from my small neighborhood elementary school to a large middle school. The only class I liked was band with Miss McDermott; her sense of humor reminded me of Mr. Cronin's, and I felt so good each time she praised me for my clarinet playing. I knew she didn't give compliments very easily.

My worst experience in seventh grade occurred each morning with young, red-headed Mr. Mikulous. At first, I thought that my homeroom teacher was just being friendly when he smiled at me a lot. But then after a few weeks, I realized that for some reason, he wasn't giving the other students the type of attention he was giving me. I had no idea why he was doing this.

Could it be that he found me attractive because my body had already developed way ahead of any of my classmates' bodies? I was still too embarrassed to ask my daddy to take me to buy a bra, so I wore my padded bathing suit top under my clothes every day to support my breasts that had developed a few years ago. There was only one other girl in my class, an overweight girl named Laura, who had breasts my size.

Early in the year, when Mr. Mikulous took attendance, he paused a bit whenever he read my name. Then he always looked up from the attendance sheet and smiled right at me. It made me feel so uncomfortable. But because he was the teacher, I knew I needed to be respectful, so I smiled back. A few months later, when he walked down the rows in the room, I felt his arm brush mine as he walked by. It seemed like he always went out of his way to go down my row, too. Often, when he gave the daily announcements to the class, he just looked at me the entire time he was talking.

For the first time in my life, I felt a creepiness about the behavior that a grown man had towards me. But I was afraid to tell Daddy because I imagined what he might do to Mr. Mikulous if he knew I was being treated this way.

In the middle of the year, I decided that since I wasn't getting a grade for homeroom, and Mr. Mikulous seemed to be getting more and more aggressive, often asking me to stay after class just to look me up and down and ask how I was doing, I would change how I acted with him and not acknowledge him at all. Maybe this would help him to stop focusing so much of his attention on me.

It worked. Within a few weeks, when I stopped looking at him for any reason and responded with just a couple of words when he called on me, always keeping my head down, he stopped looking at me, too. Afraid that his creepy behavior would return, for the remaining months of the school year I kept ignoring him.

Thankfully, it's now summer, and I'm away from him, hopefully forever.

July 1969

There isn't much to do today. Mother is back in the hospital, so I'm home by myself while Daddy is still working. Since I was eight-years old, one day each summer Daddy has taken me on the long railroad trip to the Kings County Supreme Court to be with him for his day at work. I always love sitting at his desk and hearing him swear in each witness. Because he took me to work with him last month, I have little hope of getting away from the house until he is on summer vacation at the beginning of August.

Daddy just learned that because he is sixty-two years old, he's eligible for retirement, so he's in the process of filling out all the paperwork so he can retire in a few months. He already told me that with his monthly pension and Social Security checks, we'll still have enough money each month to live. I sure hope he's right.

I've watched enough TV game shows; after a while they all start to sound the same. I switch off the TV and move it back down to its corner floor spot. Then for some reason, I decide to explore my daddy's closet—a place that I've never looked before.

I open it up. Boy, does it smell like him—a smell that is equally musty and comforting. I know that he keeps his "treasures" in some boxes on the top shelf, so I get a chair from his desk and stand on it as I reach to get the boxes down.

As I move the first box, I see a bottle with a purple and white label that has a dark red liquid in it. It looks like the type of bottle that has alcohol in it! I move my hand to reach it, and I carefully take it down from the closet shelf. It *is* a half-full bottle of alcohol! It has the name *Manischewitz Wine* on the label with some large purple grapes beneath the name.

What is Daddy doing with wine in his closet? He and Mother have always told me that real Christians don't drink alcoholic products, and the pastors in the churches I've attended all my life have said the same thing. I've heard people give their testimonies about how drinking alcohol caused them to do very bad things and ruined their lives. *What is Daddy doing with wine in his closet?*

More than any other feeling, I feel betrayed by my daddy—a person whom I've trusted more than anyone else on the earth. I take the bottle and try to open it. I don't care what Daddy will think. After a few hard tugs, I unscrew the cap, and as I do, a strong smell fills my nose, and my eyes begin to water. There is only one thing I must do with it now—get rid of it.

I walk to the bathroom, and as quickly as I can, I pour the remaining wine into the toilet bowl. A sharp smell quickly fills the room. How can Daddy drink this nasty stuff? There is no way that Daddy should have this in our house.

I don't care if he finds out that I did this. He is a liar and a hypocrite. And I'll tell him this as soon as he comes home from work.

September 1969

The saddest thing just happened. Because my brother Paul is so smart, he just left for Wheaton College in Wheaton, Illinois—Billy Graham's school. He won't turn sixteen till the end of the month, but he'll be in college with students who are three years older.

After skipping second and ninth grades and making a very high score on the SATs he took when he was fourteen, his headmaster suggested that Princeton University would be an excellent college for Paul to attend. But that school is much too worldly for my parents to approve of. They told Paul that he had to find a Christian school—one that would keep him protected from the world—and Wheaton College is it.

And now I'm even more alone.

I don't have him to talk to about the latest poem he's written or the girl he has a crush on. At Christmas last year, we were finally given some normal toys for kids our age, but now I won't have him to play Monopoly and Spirograph with anymore. I know that my daddy is planning to retire in a few months from his job in the Supreme Court so he can control Mother better during the day, but as much as I love my daddy, my best friend Paul is gone.

How can I go on without him?

September 1969
Age 12

No More

No more long walks at nighttime
No more crying, laughing, and singing with each other
No more confiding in each other in bad times
Nor more making believe we're boyfriend and girlfriend
No more trying to play chess
No more trying to play tennis
No more picking out your wardrobe
No more picking out your girlfriends
No more fighting and making up
These things have all gone away…with you.

December 1969

Yesterday, Paul came home from college for Christmas vacation. It's so great to have him home again! I've missed him so much, and he told me he missed me, too. He even wrote me a few letters when he was gone. I have them all saved in a pink-flowered cardboard box in my bedroom.

Today, Daddy, Paul, and I are going to my Aunt Rosa's house to celebrate an early Christmas with her and my Uncle Larry. Since Mother is still lying on the couch all day, she'll stay at home; besides, she hates Aunt Rosa and has yelled at her and called her a witch so many times.

Aunt Rosa is Daddy's sister, and they grew up in a large Italian family—ten kids in all. Of their siblings, she and my daddy are the closest in age to each other, and they were the only ones who walked four miles to Erasmus Hall High School each day. They have always had a special connection.

Aunt Rosa and Uncle Larry live about fifteen miles from us on the other side of Long Island, and we see them a few times each year. They have a grown son named Arthur whom we never see. Because my parents are so much older than most parents, the many cousins that we have are all a lot older than Paul and me. I have only met three of them. I wish that we could celebrate Christmas in a large family with other kids. When I've watched *The Waltons* a few times, I always get so sad that my family is so small and that my mother is so sick.

When we walk into Aunt Rosa's small ranch home, I can already smell the special Italian Christmas red sauce that she makes each year. Then I take a few more steps inside, and the strong evergreen scent of their large, decorated Christmas tree fills my senses. I wish we had a real Christmas tree like this instead of the small, fake silver one that sits upstairs on our card table. The Italian food that Aunt Rosa cooks tastes very bitter compared to Mother's spaghetti sauce. She also serves something with eel that Daddy convinced me to try one year; it tasted absolutely disgusting! I usually don't eat very much at her Christmas dinner, except for the dessert, a spumoni layer cake that I can never get enough of. Aunt Rosa also has glass candy dishes all over her house; I'm already eyeing the one that has the chocolate kisses in it.

After we say hello, Paul quickly finds his corner chair where he will sit and read magazines. He grabs one of the many *National Geographic* magazines on the coffee table. Except for when he is eating dinner with us, he won't leave that chair. Uncle Larry, who never seems happy to see us, is in his big brown chair by the door reading the newspaper.

Aunt Rosa asks me to join her in the kitchen while she finishes preparing the food for our special meal.

"What size shoe do you wear now, Christine?" she asks.

"Size eight," I tell her.

"Great. I have something special for you for Christmas that I hope you will like."

Wow. I usually don't get a Christmas present from her. What has happened to change that? I can't help but look at the many wrapped presents under the tree and wonder which one is mine.

After dinner, she hands me a large box wrapped in red paper. She tells me to open it.

When I tear off the wrapping paper and lift the lid of the box, I see a pair of the most beautiful light brown go-go boots that I have ever seen. I have seen so many girls wearing boots that look like this.

"Thanks so much, Aunt Rosa!" I give her a big hug.

I try them on, and they fit perfectly. They even have heels, something that I have never worn before.

Now I feel like I am no longer a twelve-year old girl. I have grown into a young woman. I hope that I'll soon find the courage to ask Daddy to take me to Klein's to buy me a bra.

January 1970

It has been two months, and Mother remains on the black couch in our upstairs den. When I climb up the six steps to check on her, she tells me to leave her alone. Drool constantly drips down her mouth, but she seems unaware that it is there. I have no idea what she has been drinking or eating, because when I ask her if she wants anything, she tells me that she isn't hungry. She is covered only in a white sheet, and since she is now feeling no energy and isn't able to move much, the couch is covered with weeks of her urine.

Despite the nasty smell, I'm so relieved to see her this way. By now, I know the pattern after she gets better and is released from the mental hospital. I know that she'll be in her low cycle for weeks—hopefully months—and she'll be unable to hurt me or embarrass me.

One afternoon after a long day at school, I decide once again to check on her. As I climb the steps, I hear her call out to me.

"Bring me a piece of paper, Christine."

I turn around and go back downstairs to my bedroom and tear a sheet of loose-leaf paper out of my blue notebook. I pick up a pen and re-climb the stairs.

When I see her, her head is raised up a bit from her pillow, and she tells me to bring her a Bible to write on. I pick one up from the coffee table and hand it to her with the paper and pen.

She scribbles something on the paper and hands it back to me.

I adore you
Mother

November 1970

I am now almost in the middle of eighth grade—my last year to attend Ralph J. Osgood Jr. High. I have enjoyed playing the clarinet for the past five years and have worked myself up to the first-chair position in the middle school band. Since my mother doesn't allow me to play the clarinet at home because she thinks it's a black demonic instrument, I work on my drills and other music after school each day in a practice room.

Miss McDermott, my fun band director, is one of my favorite teachers ever, and I don't want to disappoint her. Her jokes and impersonations often take my mind off what is going on in my house. My daddy has just retired, so that helps, too. Now, I'm not as worried about what my mother will do each day and about what I'll see when I get home from school.

For the first time, we have found a church that we haven't been kicked out of—mostly because this time I pleaded with Daddy to not let Mother attend this church with us. They have a very active youth group that keeps me busy with so many fun activities.

Finally, I don't feel the heavy weight of Mother's sickness on my back. And for the first time, I'm making friends who stick around since they don't know about my mother—friends I can hang out with at Sunken Meadow State Park, the beach that is close to our home, and friends who invite me to their homes.

I'm also beginning to feel attractive. Often when I walk to and from town, I hear catcalls and whistles from men that are directed towards me. Since my breasts are now developed, I still wear my padded bathing suit top under all my tops and dresses. I'm still too embarrassed to ask my sixty-two-year-old daddy to take me to a store to buy a bra, and with my mother so sick, I know that she won't take me.

But at least my breasts aren't flopping around when I walk like my mother's large breasts do.

December 1970

This past year, my mother has spent so much time in the mental hospital. It was my daddy who called the cops last month when she exposed herself to some people who were walking by our house. Once again, life is so peaceful without Mother in the house. Besides our exactly fifty-year age difference, I love hanging out with Daddy. Once I even looked up the days in June that we were born and learned that we both were even born on a Monday!

Ever since Daddy taught me to play tennis when I was eight years old, much of our time together has been spent on the tennis court. We go to church together every Sunday morning and evening and even sometimes go to the prayer meetings on Wednesday nights. When we sit in a pew at church, we always hold hands. Sometimes he even draws funny comic faces for me in the church bulletins. And when we sing one of his favorite hymns, "In Times Like These," I love how he always grips my hand extra tightly when we together sing, "My anchor holds, and grips the solid rock."

Since I was five, Daddy has ordered thousands of tiny booklets that are filled with Bible verses to help people when they need help. Throughout my childhood, I have watched him stand outside malls and arenas and give them to people as part of his Christian testimony. Several times when I was younger, I even helped him give them out, but then I started to feel uncomfortable. Thankfully, Daddy didn't make me keep giving them out.

Yesterday, Daddy told me that he has decided to create a non-profit organization called Read the Bible, Inc. that will make it possible for him to give these booklets to even more people. He told me he learned that if a non-profit organization orders the booklets from Little Bible Ministry, they are much cheaper, and he also won't have to pay taxes on them. He said that this is reason enough for him to go through the process of establishing a non-profit. Now that Mother is in the hospital, I'm in school all day, and Daddy is retired, he has so much free time. I'm glad he will have this to do so he won't get bored or feel lonely.

My daddy loves me more than anyone I know. He often kisses me on my forehead right between my eyebrows and tells me how lovely I am and that there is nothing I cannot do. His words mean everything to me. I've watched him deal with my mother for so many years, and I've gone from feeling anger at him for allowing her to always come home from the mental hospital, to feeling amazement because of his unconditional love for her.

Why did Paul and I have to deal with so much trauma during our early childhoods—situations that no children should ever experience? Yet he has stood by my mother faithfully and always reminded us that "she is your mother." When I sometimes complain to him about her behavior and tell him that I don't want her to live with us anymore, he asks, "So what do you think I should do with her, Christine? Toss her out on the street? Leave her in the mental hospital for the rest of her life to rot away? All she has in this world is us. She stood by my side and helped me for so many years before you and Paul were born. I must stand by her side now."

Somehow this makes sense. Even though it doesn't seem like our prayers for her to get better are working, I still feel that God is hearing them, and someday I will understand why all this is happening to us.

But now my mother has been released from the mental hospital again.

March 1971

The yellow forsythias around our home are already in bloom, and from the outside of our house, most people would never know that its inside is filled with the most wretched smell given off by one of the ugliest people imaginable.

Besides having a huge overhanging stomach at a height of 5'1" and weighing over 200 pounds, my mother lost her front teeth years ago. She wears snug nylon dresses each day without any undergarments beneath them. She never shaves anywhere, so long, dark hair covers her legs and hangs from her armpits. But the most disgusting hair grows on her face. She has a dark mustache above her top lip, and more dark hair grows on her chin. The drool that comes out of her mouth is one of the side effects of the Haldol which the doctors give her each time she is hospitalized. The thin, grey hair on her head is rarely combed. She wears orthopedic beige sandals which reveal her fat, misshapen feet and yellow toenails. She doesn't walk; she shuffles. Her voice is shrill and often grating. And then there are her fat upper arms that wobble with each step she takes. She already looks twenty to thirty years older than the fifty-four years that she is.

I've just returned home from school, and on the way inside, I grab the mail from our mailbox. I quickly look through it until I find the colorful magazine *Moody Monthly*. The cover announces the "School Edition." I take it to my bedroom and begin to read about the many Christian colleges—one which I might attend one day—including Wheaton College where my brother is now.

In the back of the magazine I find a white card that asks if I would like information on any of the colleges. I see that I don't even need a stamp to send it back. I check the box of several colleges, and then I notice at the bottom of the card a school called Wheaton Christian High School. I put a check next to it, not realizing that the checkmark will soon be the catalyst to change the trajectory of my life.

April 1971

When you grow up living by the ocean, you always dream of what is out there. You want more. Inside, I hear a knocking that I need to answer. A happier life is somewhere out there waiting for me; I just need to find it.

I walk home from another day in eighth grade, climb the stairs to our front porch, and open the mailbox. In it, I find a large white envelope addressed to Christine Nicolette. It has a return address of 2N120 Prince Crossing Road, West Chicago, Illinois. I have no idea who has written to me from that address.

I tear open the envelope to find a brochure on Wheaton Christian High School. It has the name Wheaton in it, so I know the school must be close to Wheaton College where my brother is now a sophomore. The school looks like such a friendly place, and when I look closer, I discover that they have a boarding program that begins in the ninth grade! Oh, wow! If only...

My daddy walks into my bedroom and asks what I'm reading. I show him the brochure.

"If only it were possible for me to go to a school like this for high school," I tell him.

"Maybe it is," he replies.

What?

He reads through the brochure and tells me how great it would be if both of his children were together again. Even though he would miss me so much if I left the house, he knows that my mother's situation is so unstable, and he has already seen the damaging effects of it on my life. And more than anything else, the possibility that I could attend a Christian high school rather than a worldly one that "is filled with kids on drugs who indulge in promiscuous lifestyles" is comforting to him.

He tells me that he will call the school tomorrow and see if they offer any scholarships as he knows we don't have enough money to pay the full price for my schooling.

I rush home from school the next day to learn that not only did Daddy make the phone call to the school, but also the man in the admissions office whom he talked to offered me a scholarship to attend the school and to live in the dorm! The man told him they could probably find me a job working in the dorm kitchen that would help pay for my boarding fees. Daddy also learned that the school is just ten miles west of Wheaton College, so it would be possible for me to see Paul easily on the train which stops in both Wheaton and West Chicago.

I am speechless. Could it really be possible for me to get away from my mother? Could it be possible for me to have a fresh start in a place where nobody knows anything about her? Just the thought of the possibility of a new life brings me hope.

August 1971
Age 14

Ten days left to wonder what it would be like
to have a mother who would cling to her daughter
who hopes to never see her mother again.

She tells me if I ever blame her for Daddy's death
she will never speak to me again.
But she constantly prays for Daddy to die
and makes his life so miserable.

"You'll get what you deserve, Mother."
And I walk out of her life and into my own.

September 1971

Since our schools both begin after Labor Day, on September 2nd, in a loaded-down car, we leave Mother to fend for herself. We drive almost 900 miles west to the beginning of Paul's junior year at Wheaton College and to the beginning of my new life at Wheaton Christian High School. I love knowing that our schools are just ten miles from each other. If I want to see Paul, I can probably find someone who lives by the college to drive me to the off-campus house where he lives.

When we finally pull up to the school, I notice that the dorm is located on the second floor of a Tudor-style large building—one that I later learn had been used as The University of Chicago's Country Home for Convalescent Children. Miss Kahlil, a friendly woman, has been waiting for my arrival and introduces herself as my dorm mom. Then she leads me up a flight of stairs to a small room that overlooks the parking lot at the front of the school. She tells me that I will have a roommate named Denise, but Denise won't be arriving till tomorrow.

I scan the tiny room. All I see are two bunk beds with thin, uncovered mattresses, two dark brown wooden desks and chairs, and one set of black wooden drawers. How can this room be large enough for both of us? It reminds me of some of the plain rooms that I had seen in the mental hospital. How I wish it had the bright yellow curtains and white furniture of my room in Kings Park!

But I am finally away from my mother. And here, nobody even knows about her. This more than makes up for it. I decide that with just a little work, I can make this room look a lot better.

September 1971

Dear Christine,
Received your joyful letter today, and I'm so happy you had such a good time on Paul's birthday. I believe God is going to do great things now for you and Paul. You have suffered for Christ for seven years, and now Praise God your suffering is over. We are getting along fine here. The Devil is conquered, Praise God. We are just at the time now before the tribulation, and God's words say, "Watch therefore for ye know not what hour your Lord doth come" Matthew 24. Luke 21 says, "Watch ye therefore and pray always, that ye may be accounted worthy to escape all these things that shall come to pass, and to stand before the Son of men." Miracles are happening every day that never happened before, and Satan will finally be defeated by the Brightness of His coming. Dear one and Paul, keep pure, read the Word, pray, and witness for Christ.

Love,
Mother

October 1971

It's a lonely Saturday because I don't have much to do. I wake up early as usual to work in the dorm kitchen helping to serve breakfast and then wash the dishes. I'm the only boarding student who works in the kitchen, but I know that if I am to stay at this school, I need to earn some spending money. Daddy sure doesn't have much money, especially now that he is retired.

After I serve the scrambled eggs to almost eighty dorm students, and it looks like everyone has been served, I get the large box of Saran Wrap to cover the pastries that haven't been taken. I wait till Gary, the kitchen supervisor, isn't looking. Then I quickly shovel a cheese danish into my mouth before I wrap the rest up. Finally, I can eat sweet foods like this! And my mom can't do anything about it.

So far, my schoolwork hasn't been that challenging. All my classes are so much smaller than they were last year. My biology teacher, Coach Mayberry, is also the wrestling coach, and all he does each day is to review the new biology terms with us for the first fifteen minutes of class; then he tells us to memorize them during the rest of class. He doesn't seem to care whether we are memorizing them or not, so most of the kids in my class just end up talking to each other.

My English class is taught by an older woman named Miss Westphal. I love to read and write, but all we have done so far are boring grammar exercises.

My favorite class is gym class with Miss Dawson. She makes whatever we do fun, and we get to play volleyball each day—a sport that I am growing to love.

I don't have much homework this weekend, so I know I can finish it after church tomorrow. A couple of weeks ago, a tall, cute guy in my English class named Mark Frost invited me to attend the church where his dad is a pastor, Church of the Open Door. Last Sunday, his brother Gene, a student at Wheaton College, picked me up and took me there. Everyone was so friendly to me! Afterwards, Mark's family invited me to join them for lunch at their house. I thought that lunch would be just for a few of us. I quickly learned that they had invited about twenty people! I felt so comfortable with this fun and loving family and already think that I may have found my church home.

But I don't feel comfortable back at school. Many of the wild kids in the dorm have started to hang out together, and I don't have much in common with them. Only one girl named Roxanne has been friendly to me, but she goes home every weekend to visit her parents who live about an hour from the school.

My roommate Denise, who never seemed to want to talk to me, got kicked out last week after they found the drugs she was keeping in a vitamin bottle in a drawer in her desk. She was always leaving our room after curfew to meet guys in the winding, steel fire escape to do who-knows-what. So many of the kids in the dorm were clearly sent here because their parents didn't know what to do with them. I guess you could say the same thing about me, too, but I sure wasn't sent here because I was getting high or making out with guys every night.

It's been so nice to have the room to myself. I finally feel like I can create a space that is just mine. I needed another chest of drawers and found one for ten dollars at a thrift shop on the campus. They also had colorful throw pillows for sale, so I bought six for my bed.

When we were in town last Wednesday, I bought some candles that I light each night when I listen to my favorite album, Carole King's "Tapestry," on the small record player Daddy bought me as a goodbye gift before he headed home. I also bought some posters of pretty outdoor nature scenes to put on the walls. Now my room has become a cozy, happy place where I love to be.

A few days ago, I learned that there is a path called the Prairie Path that runs alongside the south border of the campus. I decide that this is a good time to take my blue notebook and a pen and wander down the grassy hill to find it. It doesn't take me long to find the entrance and begin to walk on the winding, dirt path. All around me are trees whose leaves have started to turn so many beautiful fall colors.

After a while, I sit down in the grass and open my notebook. Now that I have some paper and a pen, I feel like I have a friend, and I don't feel alone anymore.

Later that night, I go for another walk. I stop and sit under a lamppost, and in the stillness I write:

The night is clear and cool.
The air is fresh and smells of wet autumn leaves.
The sky is black, except for its bright moon
which makes You seem real to me.
The stars are highlights in the heavens,
and as I sit on the cold, wet grass I think of You
and what You are doing for me.
Shivers begin to run up my spine.
The world is irrelevant—but You sure are not.

December 1971
Christmas Break
Age 14

Blue eyes meet
blue eyes
No love at all
"You are a whore and a witch, Christine"
Blue eyes see
hatred violence blasphemy rebuke
Blue eyes cry
about
blue eyes
not beautiful

January 1972

It is finally Wednesday—the day that we are taken by bus into downtown Wheaton and are given two hours to shop. I've been waiting impatiently all day for school to get out. The day has crawled by, and with each passing class, my mouth waters more and more.

I anticipate this day every week. I don't have much to buy as far as supplies or clothes go, but I love to spend just about all of the money I have earned from working in the dorm kitchen on Wednesday afternoons. In just a few hours I am going to eat every type of food that I couldn't eat in my childhood—and my mother can't do anything to stop me.

By now, I know exactly the pattern of my walk after the bus drops me off. I quickly leave the other kids who are dropped off as I need to be alone when I eat. Usually the other kids aren't ready for dinner first, so I head to Cock Robin, a burger house that is known for its great malts. I enter the store and order the usual: one large hamburger and one large chocolate malt. As it is being prepared, I feel my heart quicken. I pick it up at the counter a few minutes later and sit down at an empty table and begin to savor each sip and bite. It doesn't take me long to finish.

Next is a stop at the Swiss bakery—how I love their little cookies! I learned that I can buy them by the pound, so I enter the store and ask for a pound of their assorted butter cookies. Should I ask for two pounds today? They look so good! But I can always come back for more on the way back to the bus. The cashier rings the cookies up, and I head out, devouring my first butter cookie with chocolate sprinkles before I get out the door.

Now to window shop while I polish off the rest of the bag. I wander down to the train station and sit on a bench for a while waiting for the next train to stop. When it does, I quickly resume my walk. I have about six cookies left to go. The candy shop isn't too far from here. I'll have the cookies eaten before I get there.

I arrive at Wallace's Candy and open the door. The cookies are done, so fudge is next...and maybe a few katydids, my favorite. I'm in luck. They have just made a batch of peanut butter fudge. It looks like manna from heaven. I must get at least half a pound of it—I can have some now and take whatever is left back to my dorm room.

As I leave with the fudge, I know that there is one more thing left to buy—a double scoop of homemade ice cream at the old-fashioned ice cream parlor on Wheaton Avenue. But I need to have a bit more fudge first, so I head to the small park in the center of town where I can sit on a bench and slowly eat it while I watch the people go by. After a few minutes on the bench, I see that it's getting a bit dark, so I know I must hurry to get my ice cream. I can always take it back on the bus with me if I need to.

The chocolate ripple and rocky road sound good today—all on a sugar cone. Creamy, sweet, and divine. I finally feel complete. A perfect end to another perfect Wednesday afternoon.

February 1972

Dear Christine,
Received your wonderful letter today and I am so happy that you are adjusted so well to the school. I am hoping the Lord will give you a special gift as you are taking piano lessons. I do hope you will be able to play in church someday. After school, try to get outside and take a walk in the fresh air every day. Since you are spending so much time working in the kitchen and in the classroom, you need some fresh air. How are your chapel exercises? Is there anybody spiritual in the school? Ask God to fill you with His Holy Spirit so that you may be a light there. Are you learning well in the Bible? Are your teachers capable? I do hope that when I see you this summer that you will have grown much in the Lord and that you are getting to be a real Christian. The secret is Read, Pray, and Witness. Otherwise there is no joy in life. Are you doing any witnessing? I think that you know by this time that no show or clothes or meals or anything in the world can ever bring real joy. It's just the Holy Spirit in your heart that will fill your every need. I pray that you will be filled with a double portion. Keep on writing. I love your letters. Share this one with Paul.

Love,
Mother

March 1972
Age 14

A Prayer for You

You make me cry
because I think that God
doesn't care enough
to heal you
and make you
everything to me
that you could be.

I wipe my tears
and pray that
God will help me
to understand
and help you
to be my mom
and not to be
influenced by
the devil
whom I've
hated for
nine years.

July 1972

Dear Christine,

We just received your letter this morning, and it is so good to hear from you so often. I'm so glad you are enjoying summer camp and beautiful Pennsylvania. It is really the first time that you have attended a real camp. It's wonderful how you are adjusting yourself to being away from home so well. That year at school did so much for you.

Concerning the Enemy of our souls, he goes with us wherever we go, so we just have to listen to what God said to Paul, "My Grace is sufficient for thee." Paul, too, had a messenger from Satan to buffet him. Every child of God is hated for His name's sake. Jesus said, "If they hated me they will hate you too." So this is our cross that we must bear as Christians. Be faithful in witnessing for Him. That's what is going to count in Eternity. Now dear one, continue to enjoy your stay at camp, and take good care of your health.

Love in Him,
Mom

July 1972
Camp Beth Sar Shalom
Age 15

First Kiss
(For Danny Disantis)

They were short
but sweet

Three
of them
I thought weren't enough

And after
three strikes
you were out

(and you didn't get a chance
to be up again)

September 1972

My Dear One,

It's always a time of joy to write to you about the many items that concern us. Since you and Paul are so far away, we constantly remind the Lord that He will make His wisdom present in you. May He provide wisdom and discernment as you lead morally clean and healthy lives! No excesses or careless living. That means moderation in every area. Memorize Luke 18:27.

Mother was so sweet over the phone. However, during the day, she is taking on some of her former silly, inane antics, like touching her nose, hair, and other gestures to avert satanic curses she seems to feel. Ask Christ to finally rid her of these far-out unreasonable fantasies.

Christine, I'm selecting you to be both father and mother to Paul. He's so alone and does need the advice and encouragement of absentee parents. Try to fill this need on our behalf. Keep his spirits and confidence high. Continue to be his mainstay.

Your ever loving,

Dad

April 1973
Age 15

Could it be faith, Lord?
He and we (2 hims and i)
have watched
nothing final happen.

Could it be faith, Lord?
To make her yours again
Could it be faith, Lord?
To bring that
shine back
into her eyes
Could it be faith, Lord?

We have bowed long hours before you
Could it be faith, Lord?
That will cool her damaged dirt mouth
and take her insanity
and make it sane
Could it be faith, Lord?
Just a little faith?
Right now it
will be hard
to even get
my faith
to be the size
of a small seed...
Is that enough?

September 1973

Dear Christine,

I'm so glad we decided to take this trip to Israel. It has been a very interesting journey so far. The Devil is simply raging. He knows his time is short. I have done some witnessing to the Jews but with a new approach as the home of Jesus Christ is a stumbling block to them. So I have used a Jewish approach from the Old Testament and have found it more effective. They will know who their Messiah is by the time I leave here in three days for unfortunately they know the Devil, and they feel him from the works of the Gentiles and the Jews. We are having quite a challenge here, but that is the usual thing when I travel.

Love in Christ,
Mother

March 1974

Dear Christine,

I know you are awaiting a letter from your mother, so I am taking the time to write to you. I have been so busy putting the Devil into the Lake of Fire that I have not found time to write. We are getting very close to the end now, and I have the very Lord Jesus Christ speaking to me for some time now, just like he spoke to the prophets of old. He is the most wonderful Lord you can ever know, and I know He has spoken to you through the Holy Spirit. I have direct contact with him, however.

The Gentiles are going to suffer now just like it was prophesied in the Scriptures when He said "There are the days of vengeance." You know He was put on the cross by Satan, and He is going to get "him" for that. So be of good cheer. If your faith has to suffer now, just remember that these people were put to abide by him, namely, Sophie, Paul and Christine. Be brave as you have been in the past when your mother suffered at the hands of the Devil and when your poor, poor daddy had to take it.

Amen.

Mother

July 1974
Age 16

You are back to your
old state of mind
and like vomit
filthy words are
thrown out of your toothless mouth.

You move your hands in the air
and over your body
in a senseless way.

You stop and stare
thinking the devil is surely dead this time
and you say to me
"You'll find out, Christine."

You pray that
daddy will die
and all day and night
you curse at him and call
him a wizard.

You make him take you to
San Diego and
ask him for $29 for
a new dress and then
you curse in his face
on the way home and
say your life will be
the greatest
when he dies.

Your depression has been
exchanged for a mind
full of useless soot.

You make my bed
cook me chicken
buy me hot pink shorts
and curse in my face.

You cry out in bed because your
innocent children have become
witches and
you tell me "you're just a child—
you know nothing."

Now you want me to get out of your house
and return to my friends in Wheaton.

I can't pray anymore
God.
I'm leaving her
and my fists
in your hands.

August 1974
Age 16

God, sometimes I feel like killing her.
I try to close her curse-filled mouth by
beating her when those
ugly words come out.
"You better lay off, cause heredity might give you what I got,"
she says, and laughs.

You kicked the moneychangers out of the temple, God.
Why can't you kick the filth
out of my mother?

Daddy walks into the room
and asks me to join him in a Bible study
and prayer for my mother.
I laugh.

How can I pray for a woman who
just told me that she is going to
come at me with a knife
in the middle of the night?

October 1974

After almost four happy and life-changing years at Wheaton Christian High School, I am now just about ready to graduate. Since I have only seen my mother during the summer and on school holidays, I simply am able to fly.

While it was initially tough to be so far away from Daddy, I survived my first year away from home and ended up being one of the fourteen girls left in the school dormitory; the other girls had gotten kicked out due to their drug use or because they broke the dorm rules. The dorm closed for good in June of 1972. Thankfully, I was quickly adopted by my pastor's family, the Frosts, and I became one of the many boarders in their spacious home at 425 E. Harrison Avenue in Wheaton.

I embraced living with a large family and was so fortunate to live with this one for two years. Quickly, their youngest son Mark and I became good friends. He was the class president, and I was the class secretary—titles that we kept all four years of high school. His great sense of humor kept me laughing, and I loved watching him excel on the football field and basketball court.

His older brother, Gene, was my fun and charismatic youth group leader at the Church of the Open Door. After church on Sundays, a group of us often loaded into Gene's maroon Plymouth Sports Fury convertible and headed to Ponderosa Steak House for lunch together.

I particularly relished hanging out in the Frost kitchen late into the night and being part of a group of family members and boarders who discussed whatever theological and world issues that were on our minds. It was not unusual for me to help my caring and hilarious surrogate mom, Marie Frost, do her grocery shopping at 10 p.m.

Then during my junior year in high school, my best friend Laurie Hiller and her family, who also attended my church, asked if I could finish out high school by living with them during my senior year. I already felt so embraced by the wonderful Hiller family that I knew I had to say yes.

Now it is my senior year, and Laurie's mom, Ruth Ann Hiller, has quickly become the mom I've always dreamed of. She is kind, loving, and accomplished. She involves me in all the activities in her family, from helping with the Saturday morning cleaning, to being part of the many groups that she opens her luxurious home to.

At the Hillers, I'm given a beautiful upstairs bedroom that has white lace curtains, marble-topped, carved antique furniture, and a thick lace bedspread covering the colorfully quilted brass bed. Each school day, Laurie and I wake to Ruth Ann's sweet voice coming through the house intercom, "Girls, breakfast is ready!"

When we arrive downstairs, we find a beautifully set table, complete with freshly squeezed orange juice, hot oatmeal, vitamins, and a daily Bible verse in the upper right corner of the green place mat. Gentle music is playing from the intercom while Ruth Ann whisks around the kitchen, making sure that Laurie and I have our sack lunches ready to take with us before we head out the door. Usually I can hear the dryer going from the adjacent laundry room, which reminds me how early Ruth Ann must have been up to start getting her home ready for the day. I feel like I'm experiencing a big chunk of heaven on this earth.

These two families, as different as they could be, provide me with a foundation of support and predictability that I never had experienced. Throughout my childhood, I had often dreamed of living in homes like theirs. Now that I feel so much stability from these families, at school I am able to excel in my academic work and to dive into just about every possible extra-curricular activity. I especially cherish the time I spend singing in the concert choir, serving as secretary of our class, being the editor-in-chief of our yearbook, and being a cheerleader for the football and basketball teams.

I'm also very involved in my active church youth group where I meet more people whom I hope to keep as friends for the remainder of my life. And all the while, the absolute best part of my life is that nobody knows anything about my mother as I prove to myself each day that I am nothing like her.

November 1974

There is no college I want to attend other than Wheaton College, so it's the only school I'm applying to. It's the college that my brother Paul, my inspiring youth group leader Gene Frost, and many other people I know have attended. I've loved hearing stories about the great classes my friends have taken from professors like Dr. Webber and Dr. McClatchey. I'm so convinced this is the right school for me that I even filled out an early application last year.

I thought my mostly A's from Wheaton Christian High School would mean I would be accepted, but I got a letter back from the Office of Admissions stating that I hadn't taken enough difficult classes in high school to qualify for admission; I needed to beef up my senior year schedule so they would see that I can excel in more challenging classes, too.

My high school is so small that we don't have a guidance counselor, so I took classes that appealed to me. Nobody ever told me that I would need geometry, Algebra II, world history, chemistry, and physics! The other problem was my low SAT score. I didn't know anything about this test—just when it was given and that I needed to show up at my school and take it. So, one Saturday morning when I spent three hours taking it, I was shocked to discover that half of the math section covered geometry, a subject I knew nothing about. Of course, my math score was low—what did they expect?

This year I'm proving to the Wheaton College admissions office that I can excel in even more challenging classes. I'm taking Anatomy and Physiology right now, the most challenging class I've ever had, and it's taught by the best teacher I've ever had, Mrs. Taylor. And I'm earning an A in it. I'm also taking another year of Spanish taught by another tough teacher, Mrs. McKelvey, and I'm earning an A in that class, too, along with my A's in English, Bible, choir, and United States Government. Shouldn't that be enough to prove to the Office of Admissions that I deserve to be admitted?

January 1975

Dear Christine,

I think you are making a great mistake in not applying to Christian Heritage College in San Diego. The school was really founded on Christian principles. The enclosed brochure shows you the Christian high school that Timothy LaHaye runs. You can read Christ right in it. I know you want to be near Paul, but the Lord can put Paul and his work right here in San Diego County where it always is beautiful and the nearest place to heaven as far as climate is concerned. The college is so beautiful and the kids that study there love the Lord. You'll be lost in a larger school like Wheaton College that can never be as spiritual as a small college.

Love,
Mother

March 1975

Today has been one of the saddest days of my life. After all my hard work in and out of the classroom these past four years, I just learned that Wheaton College has rejected me. How can this be? I know it's a selective school, but I'm known in my class for being one of the brighter students, and I have shown my other strengths consistently in high school through participating in virtually every part of my school.

I've held class office four years, worked up to being editor of the school yearbook, and participated on the volleyball, track, and tennis teams. I also was a cheerleader, sang in the choir four years, and played in the band. And outside of school I have participated in every possible church experience that I could. What more do they want from me? I am so humiliated.

I call Daddy to tell him my sad news, but since he never attended college, he doesn't think that my getting rejected from Wheaton College is too big of a deal. He tells me not to worry about it—just to find another college that I can quickly apply to. But there is nowhere else I want to go! I've put all my eggs in the Wheaton College basket--I don't even know anything about any other colleges. So what should I do?

One thing I know for sure: There is no way I am going to Christian Heritage College.

April 1975

Dear Christine

Your dear mother is all better. Praise the Lord. You have to cast out the devil to get well. This time it was only four months, but that was long enough! Daddy feels better again, and we are real sweethearts. Looking forward to your graduation.

Love in our Savior,
Mother

Hello, Christine,

I never expected Mother to hang up on you the way she did since I wanted to have a closing word. So sorry about it and I can appreciate how you felt. I have been praying that by now you are calloused or toughened about her antics. Make sure you are, for there are more important things in your life than some petty behavior on her part. Just you continue to remember your duty as a prayer warrior. God's hand of blessing is ever present. So, carry on with what you're doing. Don't worry about the argument she gave and about her upsetting your closing school days. All will be ok when we get to you. It'll be a great day when I see you again. God bless you and say hi to Paul.

Much love,
Dad

June 1975

My sadness and disappointment have not left, but I must move on to another option for college. My closest friend, Laurie Hiller, and a few of my other classmates have applied to Taylor University in Upland, Indiana, a Christian college that is often considered a fallback for kids who don't get into Wheaton College. It would be great to know someone there and to continue being in school with her. Without knowing anything more than that about Taylor, I apply, and a few weeks later, I get a letter of acceptance.

I don't know what God is trying to teach me through this huge setback in my life, but whatever it is, I must learn from it and make the most from this unexpected situation.

In June, both my mother and Daddy, who during my sophomore year had moved to Escondido, California, to escape the cold Long Island winters, make the long car trip to Illinois for my high school graduation. As soon as I see Mother, my anger flares up; I know she is in her sick cycle.

I don't want her around me, let alone around my friends, as there is no telling what she will do or say. Thankfully, the situation takes care of itself as her behavior is so out of control that Daddy decides to leave her at the hotel for both the Baccalaureate service, where he has been asked to give the benediction, and the beautiful outdoor graduation service. At graduation, I sing with the select choir ensemble and am awarded the Balfour Honor Key.

My small graduating class of thirty-three feels like a family that I never want to leave.

Late June 1975

Two weeks after my high school graduation, Daddy, Mother, Paul, and I head to a Bible conference in Dunedin, Florida. For a week, Paul and I have fun socializing, singing, and studying the Bible with teens whom we had gotten to know at four past bi-annual Hebrew-Christian conferences. But then the conference ends, and we get into the car and begin the long trip to our new "home" for the summer—our parents' two-bedroom apartment in Escondido, California.

It's going to take us four days to drive across the country, and since we are in the Southern Region of the United States, and it is summer, it is already very hot outside. Due to my daddy's frugal tendencies, he has purchased a car without air conditioning.

The days are endless. Each day, Paul and I feel like prisoners in the back seat as we watch our mother's extreme antics, listen to her high-pitched voice as she constantly "curses the Devil," and try not to watch as she continues to pee indiscriminately on the seat of the car. While in the past her heavy urine scent has been repulsive, with the heat and the plastic of the car seat, the scent is now unbearable. And once again, nothing we do can make the smell go away.

Every few hours, my mother and Daddy get into screaming matches, and several times he stops the car and threatens to push her out. How I wish he would! When his threats don't work, Daddy tries to hit her into submission.

I try so hard to block the reality of this four-day trip from hell out of my mind. I spend countless hours each day resting in Paul's lap with my face turned up to his. He often reaches for my hand to hold. We both try to sleep. I dream of the ocean. Its saltwater smell and the cries of the seagulls provide me with some relief. But only for a while.

December 1975

I am barely surviving Indiana's winter. I thought Wheaton was cold in the winter, but the weather I'm experiencing here is an entirely new level of cold. The city of Upland, Indiana, is remote and small; downtown Upland doesn't even have a stoplight, just a stop sign. All around the large campus are wide open fields, perfect to whip the wind into an even greater spin. Quickly, my winter coat is not enough protection against a windchill that is often well below zero.

Not only is the cold tough to handle, but most of all, I miss my Wheaton home and family. I've made a couple of good friends at Taylor University, but I still often feel lonely and miss the beauty, quality, and culture of Wheaton. The city wasn't honored with the title of "All-American City" for nothing. I haven't given up on the prospect of someday going back there. Apparently, my daddy hasn't either.

At the end of the summer after my high school graduation, Daddy and Mother decide to move to Wheaton to be closer to me and Paul. Without my knowing it, Daddy is working to get me back to the city that has become more of a home to me than any other place I have lived.

One Wednesday night, the phone in the hall of my dormitory rings. Since nobody else is answering it, I do. It's Daddy.

"Christine, I have some good news for you. Since you couldn't be admitted to Wheaton College with your excellent academic record and the letters of recommendation of so many, I thought that as your father, I should also tell Mr. Chrouser, the Director of Admission, about you. We met this afternoon, and after talking to him, he agreed to accept you as a student at Wheaton College beginning this spring. Because the dorms are full, you'll have to live in an off-campus apartment, but you will still be considered a full-time student."

It takes me a few moments to even grasp the magnitude of what I hear—and of what my daddy has done on my behalf.

"Are you serious? I can't believe it! Oh, my God! Thank you, Daddy!"

Somehow, my almost seventy-year-old father's words had made such an impact on the Director of Admission that he agreed to take a chance on my admission. Daddy tells me he told Mr. Chrouser that he will never regret this decision.

Years later, when I am the recipient of a national teaching award, I wish I could find Mr. Chrouser and make sure he knows he made the right decision.

January 1976
Age 18

Daddy,
Keep your smile
always and shower it on me
so I can smile back
into those knowing eyes
that see through me
and tell me
that when I am sixteen
I will have more boyfriends
than I can count.
And I laugh
and say that I'm eighteen
and I've never felt
the hug of a lover.

February 1976

After completing a three-week physical science class in the short term between semesters at Taylor, I pack my suitcases and boxes. While I will miss a few of the special friends I made, everything is falling so beautifully into place for my return to Wheaton.

Since he graduated from Wheaton College in 1973, Paul has been working in Chicago writing radio spots for WMBI—Moody Bible Institute's radio station—and living in a room in an older home in Wheaton. He tells me he would love to share an off-campus, two-bedroom apartment with me. How special it will be to live with my wonderful brother!

On a Saturday in early February, Daddy drives to Upland to pick me up. As he helps me move the boxes into his car, he tells me how happy he is to know that both of his children will now be living close to his and Mother's furnished apartment. Once again, I thank him for all he did to make my admission to Wheaton possible.

A few days later, Paul and I move into an apartment at 418 North President Street—just a couple blocks from Wheaton College. We quickly enjoy sharing this space together. Even though he gets back quite late from his work in Chicago and has started to date Elsie, a girl whom I already like so much, we sometimes are able to talk and laugh late into the night. I can't wait to start my classes at Wheaton College in just a couple of weeks.

August 1977

I've just returned to Wheaton after experiencing the best three months of my life. Wheaton College mandates that all its students spend a quarter studying off-campus in one of the numerous programs that it offers throughout the world. Since I'm majoring in literature, this means that I *had* to study at Oxford University in England. Poor me, right?!

No words or pictures can ever adequately represent what it was like to take classes and travel throughout England and then later to France and Wales with the most wonderful group of sixty students who have become my friends. And I now even have a coterie of six closer friends who I can't wait to invite over to my apartment for dinner.

This was my first time to travel over an ocean, and I admit that the plane ride was tough. Sitting for the eight-hour flight was hard enough, but when the plane hit turbulence for a long time in the middle of the Atlantic Ocean, I started to feel sick to my stomach and was convinced that we were going to crash into the ocean. Thankfully, we didn't. But one thing is certain: I sure would go through turbulence again if it meant I could take another trip out of the United States.

For the first two weeks of the program, I and the other girls traveling with me boarded at the YWCA in London. After seeing the sites in London, we traveled to the famous nearby cities of Cambridge, Salisbury, Bath, and Stratford-upon-Avon. I even celebrated my twentieth birthday at Wimbledon with a few friends; it was awesome to see Bjorn Borg play Vitas Gerulitis on grass courts!

When we arrived at Oxford's gorgeous campus, I was given a small room of my own at St. Anne's College. Each weekday we spent about four hours in classes taught by all-male Oxford professors. Most of them were long lectures that required me to take copious notes. I confess that as much as I love to study literature, it was sometimes tough to sit through these long classes. But it was worth it because the best part came every weekend when we loaded into a bus and explored the places where the English literature that we were studying was written. Among the many places that we traveled were to the Lake District to see the remains of Tintern Abbey and to Dover Beach after we read Matthew Arnold's famous honeymoon poem.

I learned very quickly that Oxford served way too much food. After a huge breakfast each morning, came mid-morning tea, always served with delicious pastries. Around noon was a yummy lunch. Then there was afternoon tea, served with a variety of cookies, which came before dinner, always an elaborate four-course affair.

After eating like this for just a few days, my clothes were fitting tighter, so I knew I had to figure out a way to eat less. I decided to skip dinner every night and instead, to walk around the gorgeous Oxford campus and city. Wherever I walked, I saw cute guys with beards and wire-rimmed glasses riding their bicycles with their book bags on their backs. I heard church bells chiming every fifteen minutes. And because it was summer, colorful flowers were blooming everywhere, especially in the window boxes in front of just about every house window. This was a city of great quality without pretension.

August 1977
Oxford, England
Age 20

As I think of where my future may take me, I hope it will be to a place like this:

1. Teaching high school literature in either a Christian or secular school. Getting to know the kids and having them see Christ in me. Also using my gift of counseling.
2. Being married to a God-honoring man. Being faithful to him, caring for him, doing things together like playing tennis, going for walks, and getting dressed up and going out.
3. Being a mother who is an example of Christ, in, as well as outside, the home.
4. Having an open house to help people who need a place to stay. Being hospitable always.
5. Raising sons and throwing the football and playing tennis with them.
6. Being actively involved in a church.
7. Getting and staying attractive despite the years. Using my aesthetic sense to make this happen.
8. Playing the piano and singing often.
9. Having a backyard to roam in that has a garden, swing, and hammock.
10. Maintaining my love and need for deep talks...especially by a fireplace on winter nights.
11. Meeting and ministering to non-Christians and being able to be used to win some to the Lord.
12. Gaining knowledge about a lot--reading a lot and being more world-oriented.
13. Possibly publishing a book on my mother's illness or publishing some of my poems.
14. Not letting getting old scare me.

Christmas 1977

Dear Christine,
(Long unrecalled:
Walktalking
You listen
with patient faithful hope;
understand
and let me put on bandaids.)

Sing to the King!
Fly the strong wings
of the Dove!
For He newborn is yours...
Likewise my love.

Your brother,
Paul

December 1977

To say that both my high school and college years are spent in two very conservative Christian environments is a great understatement. But after the great turbulence of my childhood, I welcome eight years of living in the "Wheaton bubble"—a stable environment where most of my life centers on going to classes and to church activities.

Unlike Wheaton Christian High School, Wheaton College is a very challenging school for me academically. I work hard to earn the many Bs that I earn, with an occasional A and C+ thrown in. It's evident that while I learned a great deal about myself in high school and gained so much confidence from excelling in a wide range of areas, I have more than met my match at Wheaton College; seemingly everyone around me is a bright, hard worker and a committed Christian who wants to make the world a better place.

During my junior year, to earn some extra money I get a job as a waitress at a local pizza parlor named Barone's. In no time at all, I love this job and anticipate the four evenings a week that I work there. Meeting so many people who are radically different from those I am around on the Wheaton campus is so fascinating—especially after sitting in my academic classes all day.

I'm finally "in the world," and I'm even learning how to serve up beer by the pitcher. I learn that to earn good tips, all I need to do is to show off my "Best Personality" that I was voted by my class my senior year in high school. And because I get to walk so much when I waitress, I'm finding it easier to keep trim, even when I'm around yummy pizza and Italian dishes. And the best part? Bringing home money every night. Due to the grants that pay for my education and the Social Security checks that pay for my housing, for the first time in my life I can buy clothes I like, even if they aren't on sale.

Early in my junior year a nice guy named Karl whom I have waited on at Barone's a few times asks me if I will go to the Fireman's Winter Ball with him. I am stunned, as I have no idea what to say. I mean, he probably is a non-Christian, and I know I'm not supposed to date non-Christians. What if it leads to more? I tell him that I will get back to him the following week.

I return to my apartment and call my good friend Diane and tell her what just happened. She ends up coming over, and we talk late into the night about the ethics of my dilemma. I sure don't want to turn Karl down and hurt his feelings! It's just one date, not a marriage proposal. Karl seems like a nice enough guy—not someone who would get fresh with me. Maybe if he isn't a Christian, I can tell him more about Christ and lead him to salvation! I decide to say yes.

I know I'll need a special dress for the occasion, so I drive to Loehmann's, a discount venue for designer clothes. I find a light blue long dress that fits, but not too snugly; I sure don't want to entice him.

Karl picks me up in his red Mustang on Saturday, December 10th. When I open the door of my apartment to greet him, I could tell that he is just as nervous as I am.

"You look so nice, Christine. How are you?"

I can feel my hands shaking a bit as I manage to say, "Fine, and you?"

We make small talk as he drives me to the Glen Ellyn decorated VFW hall where the ball is held. The first thing I see when we walk in is a large bar area. Already many people are gathered there drinking and laughing.

Karl asks me what he can get me to drink. Since I've signed the mandated Wheaton College pledge, I cannot drink any alcohol while I'm enrolled there. I tell him that a glass of lemonade would be great.

A few minutes later, he comes back, and we sit together awkwardly at a table. Eventually, he sees some of his friends and introduces me to them and to their dates. There is a band playing some loud music.

"Would you like to dance?"

"I'm sorry, but the pledge that I had to sign to attend Wheaton College not only keeps me from drinking alcohol, but it also forbids me from doing any social dancing."

He is aghast.

I feel like we are two eighth-graders at our first school dance, but I'm not even allowed to dance.

The night slowly drags on as each of the firefighters is introduced. When Karl's name is called, I clap extra loudly and hoot for him; at least I can support him in this way.

Karl drives me home, and we don't say much to each other in the car. The entire way, I'm hoping that he won't try to kiss me goodnight. I know that this would be too far to go so soon with someone who probably isn't a Christian.

As he pulls into my apartment parking lot, I start inching for the door.

"Thanks so much for inviting me tonight, Karl. I had a really nice time."

I open the car door and get out before he can even lean over.

"Good night," I hear him say.

I never see Karl again.

December 1978
Age 21

My endless checklist (a committed Christian)
of expectations (very intelligent)
in my man
somewhere (athletic) out there.
Why does (musically inclined)
so much have to matter?
Will I ever be able
to give up anything
from my list (a gentleman)
to ensure (takes care of himself)
that I get married?
Should I settle (organized)
for eight out of thirteen?
I am at the (goal oriented)
point where I (aesthetically aware)
can't imagine a (tall)
man out there who has
(internally strong)
these qualities and is
capable of loving me enough.
(knows how to ask questions)
Am I really asking
for too much, God?
(has a sense of humor)

May 1979

By the time I graduate from Wheaton College, I have been a member of their fabulous concert choir, have spent an idyllic summer with my friends studying literature at Oxford University, and have excelled in my education classes. Student teaching at Wheaton North High School during my final quarter at Wheaton is certainly the highlight; for twelve weeks, I'm finally able to apply all that I've learned when I take over all five of Miss Wood's classes and teach 125 sophomores and juniors each day.

By my senior year, I also have a cohesive group of friends I love to hang with, and I often invite them over to my off-campus apartment for what they call "Chris Nic Time." Usually this means that we sit around and discuss topics like: What do you think you will be doing ten years from now? Describe yourself from your mom's perspective. What kind of person can you see yourself married to someday? Name something that you wish that you could do to make the world a better place.

How I love to talk deeply with my friends!

Unfortunately, I learn early in my senior year that due to the tough economy and many teacher layoffs in the state of Illinois, after I graduate, it will probably be impossible for me to find a job teaching in the Wheaton area.

In early November, my good friend Eric invites me and a few other friends to spend Thanksgiving break with his family in Dallas. We drive down to his parents' beautiful home in Highland Park and spend five days seeing the Dallas sites and laughing together. The weather is perfect. All around his house, the trees are turning shades of red and gold, and I even get to play tennis outside in November.

Eric's parents are so friendly and hospitable, but so is everyone else we meet. I ask around and learn that the job market in Texas is very strong. Maybe I should consider getting a teaching job here! Two of my good friends from Wheaton, Glenn and Leslie, will even be living in Dallas after I graduate. The more I think and pray about it, the more it seems like this geographic change is probably what I need to make next.

In late May, the idea of moving to Dallas is solidified. Eric's kind parents, Martha and John Binion, write and tell me that I am welcome to stay with them until I find a place to live, so the decision to move to Dallas is that much easier to make.

Since my brother Paul insisted on giving me his 1971 Ford Pinto after he married Elsie in August of 1978, I'll even have the wheels to take me to Dallas. Even though his Pinto isn't in the best shape, it has enough juice left to make the long trip.

By the morning of June 4th, I have everything I'll need for the next few days packed into my small car, and I'm ready to go. Daddy has arranged for professional movers to deliver my furniture, piano, and other items as soon as I know where I'll be living.

It should take me about fifteen hours to make the over 900-mile drive. I'm too scared to stay in a hotel overnight by myself, and I know that if I drink enough coffee, I can stay awake for the long trip.

Feeling both excited and nervous, I leave my apartment driveway for the last time at 5 a.m. on a Monday morning. I've never done anything like this by myself before, but I know that God will be with me each mile of the way.

It's a very long drive. I try not to stop too many times because I know that it will make the drive even longer, but a couple of times, I stop driving just so I can walk around the rest areas and stretch my legs. I realize I need to have things to do to pass the time, so I decide to spend some time praying for everyone I know. I start with my immediate family and then branch out and out. Before too long, I'm praying for each student who I taught when I did my student teaching.

Then it occurs to me that I'll be moving to a place where only a few people know me. I'll be meeting so many new people and establishing my identity all over again. Who do I want to be? I have always disliked it that almost everyone shortened my name to "Chris." Not only did it sound like a boy's name, but it also didn't sound like me. When I arrived at Wheaton Christian High School in 1971, and the first person started calling me Chris, the name stuck, and before I could do anything about it, Chris was what everyone called me.

I now have the power to change this. I decide that I will introduce myself to everyone as "Christine;" the moment a person shortens my name to Chris, I will very nicely correct him or her.

By the time I arrive at the Binion's home, it's 8:30 p.m. They have been waiting for me and welcome me warmly. They show me to my accommodations in their large guest house and ask if I've eaten dinner. Once again, a fabulous Christian family has opened its arms to me, and I am the blessed recipient of the hospitality.

The following day, I drive to the Dallas Independent School District personnel office and apply for a job teaching high school English. Miraculously, immediately after taking an analogy test and being interviewed, I learn that I'm hired. Mrs. Shaw, the kind woman who interviews me, tells me that because of my excellent credentials and warm personality, I'm hired for the one English position that they have available: teaching English as a Second Language and Correlated Language Arts at North Dallas High School, an inner-city school with all the inner-city challenges that come along with it.

I won't start my job until the end of August, but I'm so thankful to have found my first teaching position so quickly. There is no doubt in my mind that this move to Dallas is a move that has God smiling.

June 1979

Since the Binions insist that I live with them until my apartment is available, I feel like I have some stability in my new Dallas life. Life at their home reminds me so much of my senior year in high school when I lived with the Hiller family. Each morning, after John Binion leaves the house to serve as a doctor of internal medicine, Martha makes breakfast, and then we pray and enjoy eating breakfast together. I feel so loved and accepted by her and am so grateful to have her presence in my life during this time of transition.

We also converse about my friend, her son, Eric, who was a year ahead of me at Wheaton College and now serves as a missionary in Swaziland, Africa. Once again, I see how wonderful it is to be part of a family who has made their faith in God and love for each other such a high priority.

Two weeks later, my apartment is finally available, so I say farewell to the Binions and drive the five miles north to the largest apartment complex in Dallas, The Village, also known as "Swinglesville" due to the hundreds of free-spirited, single people who live there.

I climb the stairs to my second-floor efficiency apartment and enter the sunny room that will now be my home. It is a room of less than 600 square feet that includes a patio overlooking a very noisy pool. As I walk in, I see the small galley kitchen to my left. I'll need to buy some bar stools to have a place to eat on the kitchen counter.

I've drawn up a diagram of where I'll place all my furniture. The large room will contain my single bed by night; many throw pillows will convert my bed into a couch by day. There's enough room for my desk to be against one wall and my upright piano to be against another. My stereo will be placed on some shelves in one corner. In the rear of the room is a sterile, normal-sized bathroom. I'll need to buy some accessories to give it personality.

Daddy has arranged for my furniture to be delivered, and thankfully by mid-afternoon, a United Van Lines truck pulls up beside my apartment building. Two men get out and begin to carry everything up the stairs to my apartment. They struggle a bit with my black upright piano, but since it was a gift that Daddy found in a moving sale, I couldn't leave it in Wheaton. I find so much joy from my piano playing.

My starting teaching salary is $10,500, and I've already calculated that my take-home pay each month will be around $500. With my monthly rent being $185, and my need to buy a more dependable car, I know that I'll need to supplement my teaching pay in some way. I plan to find a job waiting tables until school begins, and if I can juggle both jobs, I hope to keep working part-time during my first year teaching.

That afternoon, I begin to unpack. I hang up my clothes in the closet and then set up the kitchen. When I'm done, I find the boxes that have the sheets to put on the bed and towels to put in the bathroom. By the time I get into bed, it's almost 11 p.m., and I'm exhausted.

I'm sound asleep when I'm awakened by loud banging on my door and voices yelling, "*Fire! Fire! Get out!*"

I startle out of bed and look out my window. To my horror, I see large flames coming from the window of the apartment building to my right. I hear people screaming and see several people running. My heart begins to pound as I rush to put some shoes on and grab my purse. I glance at my clock radio on the way out. It's 2:00 a.m.

As I leave my apartment, I see the fire is spreading very quickly, and the fire department hasn't arrived yet. It looks like the flames are just a few feet away from my building.

I tear down the stairs and rush to my Pinto. *Where will I go?*

I turn the ignition on. At this hour in the morning, there is only one place I can go. I get on Central Expressway quickly. Thankfully, the highway is quite empty. I make my way down to Drexel Drive in Highland Park. I'm sure the Binions are sleeping, but if I could wake them, I also know that they'll calm me down and know what I should do next.

I arrive at their house, pull into their driveway, and get out of my car. When I reach their back door, I find John waiting for me; he had woken up when I pulled into the driveway, and he recognized my car.

I fall into his arms. My body is shivering, and tears are streaming down my face.

He holds me tight. "Are you okay? What happened, Christine?"

I tell him about the fire, and his first words are calming. He tells me that probably everyone was able to get out safely, and if I lost anything, it was only something material that could be replaced. But I think of all my beloved photo albums in those still unpacked boxes and of the many journals that I've kept since I was in middle school—these things are irreplaceable. I can't worry about them. Right now, all of this is out of my control.

John takes me upstairs to one of their guest rooms and tells me to get a few hours' sleep. We will talk more in the morning.

The next morning, I wake and come down the stairs to find John and Martha already sitting at the breakfast table. They're listening to the news on TV, and John invites me to sit down.

"There is good news and bad news, Christine. I just saw a segment of the news that showed that the fire only destroyed one apartment complex, which means the fire department put it out before it got to your adjacent building. But one person did die in the fire. The police arrested a man seen running from the apartment when the fire started. The man just confessed that he had gotten into a big fight with his boyfriend, tied him to the couch, and then set the couch on fire."

There is no doubt Christine Elise Nicolette is not living in Wheaton anymore.

In August 1979, I begin what will eventually be a thirty five year career teaching high school English. I learn that my teaching load will consist of five classes comprised of 135 primarily Hispanic and black teens who come from the lowest socio-economic backgrounds. Eventually, I learn that the immigrant student population at North Dallas High School is represented by over thirty countries. For the first time in my life, I am exposed to a stark dose of the real world. I am finally out of my twenty-two-year religious bubble.

August 1979 to May 1982

I spend the next three years immersing myself in both teaching and dating. Teaching comes naturally to me. I especially love helping this diverse group of first-generation kids hone their reading and writing skills and then assisting them as they apply to college, something that usually isn't on their radars.

Dating, on the other hand, is an area that I'm not too familiar with. At Wheaton College, I had gone out with a few guys on dates, but nothing resembling a serious romantic relationship ever developed. Wheaton wasn't like most colleges; because of its strict behavioral pledge its students signed, in all my years at Wheaton, I never even saw one beer can anywhere near the campus. Guys generally were more afraid of the opposite sex than anything else; if you just held hands with a guy, it was considered a big deal and one to worry about as you were beginning to go down "the slippery slope" of sexual behavior that was "an abomination to the Lord" if you weren't married. Needless to say, at the age of twenty-two, I was still a virgin.

But now my environment couldn't be more different. On the first day of in-service at North Dallas High School, I'm approached by several young male teachers and am addressed as "Hot Stuff" and "Sexy"—names that offend me. I'm invited to attend a party at the home of a teacher named Pat Barnhill that Friday night, and while there, a charismatic chemistry and physics teacher named Nim Batchelor shows an interest in me—so much so that we talk for quite a while. When he discovers that I play tennis, he asks if I will join him on the tennis court early the next morning.

Like in my parents' case, this tennis date is the beginning of a serious relationship—in our case, one that lasts over three years; it even survives when he leaves Dallas to study philosophy at The University of Nebraska's graduate school. One reason our relationship continues is because his parents and two siblings welcome me into their home and quickly become yet another loving surrogate family to me.

While Nim is gone, we rationally decide that we both should be able to date other people as there is no telling where our relationship will ultimately go. One of the most appealing of my colleagues whom I begin to date is a brilliant black poet named Tim Seibles. We are the junior and senior AP English teachers, and we have a great time creatively designing a curriculum that allows both the high-level juniors and seniors to have each of us as their teachers throughout the year. He also helps me coach the school's tennis team. We enjoy many magical moments both in and out of the classroom.

By 1982, I have more than made up for my protected life with the opposite sex.

And Daddy and Mother during this time? They move back to Escondido, California in 1979. Over the next three years, my mother resides in apartments and mental hospitals in both California and in Israel, where she and Daddy adventurously move for over a year.

Thankfully, Mother is totally on the periphery of my life. It doesn't matter how sick she is or whether she is in or out of a mental hospital. I'm coming into my own, and for the first time in my life, I feel like an attractive and confident sexual woman—a young woman who scares the shit out of her mother every time she sees her daughter.

It feels so good to finally be the one who causes her to fear.

August 1980
Age 23

Aimlessly placing red
ink on loose leaf paper
(run-on sentences fragments dangling participles poor usage)
Who gives a damn?
My thoughts wander back
to the fragment of time
we spent together
and the proper usage
we gave to it.
That's my kind of grammar.
I miss it as I do you.

April 1981
Age 23

I am afraid of myself.
There is no limit to what I could do.
Once I left my cage
I discovered a world that had been ignored
because of ignorance and conformity.
I liked this world and
sought to explore it again and again.
Each time my trip took me
further into this country.
Going back to my cage seemed less and less desirable.

Now I've done it.
I've crossed the line of no return.
Absurdity of absurdities.
Wonder of wonders.
I am old.
I am beyond belief.
I am at home in this new world.

May 1981
Age 23

Yes, I understand now.
I don't want to be a dried-up sixty-five
knitting in my rocker and
thinking about what
could have been at twenty-three.
No.
I want to sing sweet memories
of a youth full of mysteries,
aching with delight.
I want to smile from my rocker
as I think of my ideals
crumbling slowly away.
I want to grin from ear to ear
as I think of my confused head
my empty bed
and how I loved every minute of it.

Father's Day 1981
Age 24

To Daddy

Just yesterday I liked being your baby girl.
You held my hand in church and
slipped me money for the offering plate.
You fed the tennis ball to my forehand.
I thought I was second to Chris Evert.
You watched me in every band and choir concert
never mentioning the mistakes.
Your warm hazel eyes looked through me.
I couldn't escape.
I didn't want to.
You ironed my shirts and skirts and
cooked when nobody else could.
You smiled when I couldn't smile and
told me not to think so hard.
I listened when you spoke.
Your bulging biceps added to the message.
You cried when I fell off my bicycle.

Today I find myself not needing you.
I make my own money for the plate and
know I'll never have a strong backhand.
I no longer sing or play those songs and
often find myself pulling out the ironing board.

I seldom eat at home and when I do
I know how to cook for myself.
I force myself to smile when I can't and
I tell myself not to think so hard.

Sometimes, just for a moment
I wish I could feel your dry palms in mine.
Sometimes, on days like today
I wish I were still your baby girl.

June 1981
Age 24

Delivery

Today I bore a fifteen-pound baby.
I bore down on
the pages of uncertainty
like a crusader in her final hours of glory.
But it didn't help.

The baby came out wrapped in blood
without breath
so still
tied in cords of doubt and denial
numb to her world.

The sickly smiling doctor tried a slap.
Nothing.

Only the sun can explain the
why's, how's, and now what's.

July 1982

When she isn't in the manic cycle of her mental illness and cursing back the devil in people through her offensive gestures, my mother always lives an insular life—except for when she is evangelizing. Now, Mother gets another wild idea in her head. This time, it isn't about demons or putting white marble on the front of her house. She decides that God has told her that her mission is to move to Jerusalem, not just to visit Jerusalem like she did a few years ago. This way, she could convert all the Jews to Christianity.

Somehow, she convinces Daddy to join her in her mission to proselytize, so at the seasoned ages of sixty-five and seventy-four, my parents pack their life possessions in a few suitcases and move from their furnished apartment in Escondido, California, to Jerusalem, Israel.

After they are settled in yet another furnished apartment and have happily lived there for over a year, Daddy convinces me that Jerusalem is such a spectacular place that I must visit them during my summer break from teaching. He sends me almost $1000 for the plane fare on El Al, and after visiting my friends Erika and Tim in Pennsylvania, I know I must swallow my fear of flying. I cross the Atlantic Ocean without knowing anyone sitting around me and endure the almost eleven-hour flight to Jerusalem.

Thankfully, Daddy is waiting for me at the airport. It's so great to see him again! But I hadn't realized how far his arthritis has progressed. He is using a cane to walk now, so I force myself to slow down and give him my full attention.

As we walk outside, hot, dry air hits me. Daddy quickly flags down a taxi. A Mercedes-Benz taxi pulls up.

After we get my bags and our bodies in, Daddy turns to me and says, "I was hoping that you would find Mother well, but unfortunately, in the last few days, she started to be bothered by her demons again. She had been well for so long, Christine. We have shared so many months of happiness here. When you and I started to plan this trip, she was still well. I'm so sorry. Maybe your being here will snap her back to better mental health."

This is not what I was expecting. The last letter that Mother had written to me sounded like she wasn't affected by anything other than her obsessively zealous flavor of Christianity. If she is sick, I don't want any part of it; how I wish that I could get back on a plane and return to Dallas right now!

As the taxi makes its way through dusty and crowded streets to my parents' apartment, I look at the soldiers standing on every street corner proudly holding their weapons and at the barren, colorless world around me. It's hard to imagine that this country was the birthplace of God's Son.

Age 25

Two entries from my Jerusalem journal:

Monday. It is so very difficult to be here with Mother sick. She awoke in the middle of the night and started ranting and raving about what a whore I am and how evil Daddy is.

I wish I didn't hate her so much.

It is obvious that she has already done damage in the fifteen months she has lived here as nobody has called or visited. Why does she continue to be this way? With all of Daddy's prayers and saintly ways you would think that something would happen to change her. It is best for my faith that I don't see her for too long.

This morning I longed to go back to Dallas as I realized I had nobody to sightsee with. Daddy tried his best for a while; it is so frustrating when he can't walk. Why did I get the parents I have? Certainly, something special must be lying ahead for me because my family background is so unusual.

Daddy will probably be going back to the United States with me. I don't know how he can do this, as he will be leaving his mentally deranged wife 6,000 miles from home—but that doesn't seem to concern him. He has had enough of her. She will have to figure out how to fend for herself in this country that she wants so much to live in. He says he must leave because he needs care for his arthritis, but clearly that is only part of the reason. If my Mother was well...if only...

I'm so sick of this situation. I feel no love for her—only animosity. This concerns me as she is the only person in the world that I manifest this feeling towards. But, God, do you blame me?

Friday. During the past few years I've come to believe that there are certain qualities that all people should have if they are to be truly good people. These qualities are open-mindedness, a lack of bigotry and dogma, and a willingness to listen to people and to support and encourage them. The reason that it's so very difficult for me to feel anything positive for Mother is because she embodies everything that I have learned to despise. She is close-minded, dogmatic, prejudiced, harsh, crude, unloving, and critical of most people. And while here, I have once again spent some wonderful time with my daddy. He represents what I aspire to be now and at age seventy-five.

Have I ever seen someone with or even without his great pain who has such a sweet spirit, warm smile, and contagious attitude of YES to the world? I simply don't know how in his circumstances he can do it. But I know he begins each day by saying the Bible verse, "This is the day that the Lord has made; we will rejoice and be glad in it." And he loves to quote a verse from the book Philippians that says, "I can do all things through Christ who strengtheneth me."

But I still don't understand how it's possible for him to keep his spirits up each day. The world needs so many more people like him. I hope that I can someday be a mirror of him in many ways. So, the question arises: What on earth is he doing married to my mother?

October 1982

I meet Scott Gonzalez through his brother Dennis, who is my colleague at North Dallas High School. One day at lunch in the school cafeteria, Dennis asks me how things are going with my long-term boyfriend, Nim. I tell him that after many years of trying to figure out if there is a future in our long-distance relationship, we've decided to just be friends.

Then Dennis tells me he has a younger brother who has just moved back to the Dallas area after attending school in Oregon, and he wants us to meet.

I quickly respond, "I'd love to meet any brother of yours."

Dennis is truly a Renaissance man as he's a multi-lingual artist and musician. For years I have seen what a loving husband and father he is to his family.

So I can meet his brother, he invites me to a Friday night Halloween party at his house. In a crowded room, I see a guy who resembles Dennis looking through some record albums. After making my way up to him, introducing myself, and trying to make small talk, it's clear that Scott isn't interested in talking to me or to anyone else for that matter.

After the party, Dennis continues to bug Scott to ask me out. Finally, just to get him off his back, Scott acquiesces, and in early December he gets my phone number from Dennis and calls.

My high school friend Laurie, who's been living with me for a few weeks until she finds an apartment in Dallas, picks up the phone.

"Hello?"

I watch as she listens to the caller. I hear her say, "Just a minute. I'll get her." Then she turns to me with a big smile on her face and exclaims, "Chris, it's Scott!" She clearly has remembered my interest in him.

My heart beats a bit quicker as I pick up the phone.

"Hello?"

"Hello, Christine. This is Scott Gonzalez. I'm calling because I'll be going to The Who concert on Saturday night, and I wondered if you'd like to meet me afterwards for some coffee."

Wow. What kind of invitation was this? Was he going to the concert alone? But I'm so happy he called that I can't help but respond positively.

"Sure. That sounds good. Where and when should we meet?"

"Why don't we meet at a place called The Wine Press in Oak Lawn. I think they serve coffee as well as wine. Is it okay if I call you after the concert ends and let you know when we can meet up?"

"Sure."

We hang up, and I turn to Laurie, who is still grinning.

Scott calls at 9:45 p.m. on Saturday night and asks if meeting him at 10:15 p.m. would be too late.

"Of course not," I lie. I've never started a date that late, but who cares? This is the guy I'd been hoping to meet, and finally I'll have the opportunity to get to know him better.

A half hour later we meet at a cozy table for two in the small café and make the mistake of ordering chocolate coffee, something we later agree is one of the most disgusting drinks we've ever tried. But as we begin to talk, it doesn't take us long before we both know we are talking to someone special.

We discuss our mutual passion for traveling and teaching. He recently returned from a summer spent backpacking through Europe, and I had spent two weeks that summer visiting my mother and daddy in Israel. A few months ago, he transferred from Oregon State University to North Texas State University where he now is pursuing a degree in English and is getting his teaching certification; I'm in the middle of my third year of teaching high school English.

But most importantly, we discuss our Christian upbringings. He tells me about what it was like to be raised in a Mexican Baptist church—the church he still attends with his family each Sunday. As I've been on a quest to understand where God fits into my out-of-the-religious-bubble life, for the past few years I had stopped attending church. But I miss having time each week to look up, to sing some hymns, and to learn more about the Higher Power that I still know exists.

A few hours later, Scott walks me to my car. When we get there, he turns to me with a grin and says, "Okay. I've asked you out. If you want to go out with me again, you'll have to ask me out."

We say good night to each other, and I begin to drive back to my apartment. I know I'm up for the challenge of planning our first long date. It occurs to me that I've finally met someone who has the right balance of secular and spiritual; if he asks me to, I can go to a rock concert with him on a Saturday night and then attend a church service with him on Sunday morning.

This is the man I'm going to marry.

And I'm right. One afternoon when Scott has driven back to Dallas after attending a week of classes at North Texas State University, we are in my apartment's kitchen kissing. Suddenly, he pulls away from me, looks directly into my eyes, and asks in a very serious voice, "Will you marry me?"

I giggle. I mean, we have known each other for a little over two months. I had been in long-term relationships that I struggled with for years to figure out how they fit into my life, and now this question?

But my life is finally making sense, and as I'm getting to know this spectacular human being better, I already know what I feel for him is unlike what I've ever felt for anyone else—simply, I am falling in love with him.

For over two months, we have attended his church together, and I've gotten to know the remainder of his fun-loving and welcoming family. I've also learned more about his personal life and the tragedy he experienced when his beloved father, an acclaimed principal in the Dallas Independent School District, committed suicide in 1980.

With seemingly irrational words, I respond to his spontaneous proposal.

"What do you think?"

April 1983

I can't help but often glance down at my left hand and the sparkling diamond ring that Scott and I designed—tangible proof that I'm engaged to the most amazing man whom I started to date just four months ago. And now Scott and I are flying "home" to meet my parents, who are living in Escondido again. I had written to them about Scott and shared what an unusually gifted human being he is—and he is a Christian on top of everything else, which Nim and most of the other guys I had dated in Dallas were not. But he is also Mexican American, and I suspect that with her extreme mental illness and prejudice, my mom will have a problem with the fact that he isn't from "pure white blood," as she described herself to be.

After we fly to San Diego on an extended Easter weekend, we rent a car and make the fifteen-mile drive north to Escondido. My daddy has given me the address to the apartment complex where they live, so when we get close, we parallel park on the street and get out of the car. As we meet up on the sidewalk, Scott notices how quiet I am and reaches for my hand. He points to the building where they live. I feel my body go stiff, and with each step I take towards it, I feel myself shaking a bit more. We cross the street. They live in a downstairs apartment at the front of the building, and we find the apartment number quickly.

I take in a deep breath and ask Scott, "Are you ready?"

He nods.

I knock lightly on the door and hear footsteps. Daddy has been waiting for us, and in a few seconds, he opens the door with the warmest "Hello!" We meet in a hug, and I introduce him to Scott.

In my periphery, I see my mother in the background in the small kitchen that is attached to the living room. She takes a few steps forward and stops. She looks at both of us, and then she exclaims in a shrill voice, "He looks just like your other boyfriend, Nim!"

The next thing I see is that she is once again "stopping the curse." She pulls up the front of her nylon dress and exposes her bare, overhanging stomach and slightly haired private parts. Then I watch in horror as she spreads her hairy legs and emits her "holy water" all over the kitchen floor.

Oh my God! This can't be happening!

I turn and run out of the apartment as fast as my legs will take me.

A few minutes later, Scott opens the door of their apartment and motions for me to come back in. He pulls me to him and whispers, "It's going to be okay. I love you."

Reluctantly, I enter their apartment again. He takes my hand and leads me to the kitchen table, which is set with white plates, napkins, and forks. Oh, yeah...they had invited us over for lunch. How can I eat anything after my mother has just exposed herself to my future husband and then urinated on the kitchen floor?

"Sit down, Christine," Daddy says. "Everything is going to be okay. Your mother has been cooking her famous one-pan lasagna all morning and is excited to share it with both of you."

Mother has now proceeded to move the skillet to our table where she begins to spoon what looks like a large, messy concoction onto our plates. My stomach turns over as I look at the heap of corn, overly-cooked noodles, cheese, ground meat, and tomato sauce.

I play with my food on the plate. I turn to Scott, and he nods as he picks up his fork and takes his first bite. If it gags him, he doesn't show it. He beings to politely eat the mess of food on his plate.

I listen to my daddy and Scott make small talk. I look at my mother, who is eyeing Scott's every move, waiting for him to move his hand to his head or face so she will have proof that he, too, is a demon who is cursing her. Thankfully, I had warned him to keep his hands in his lap or at his side at all times so he will not be suspect. The meal progresses at a snail's pace, and I don't say much. I refuse to look at my mother.

"Have some more," Daddy tells Scott.

"No thanks, we had a big breakfast this morning, so I'm not very hungry."

After what seems like endless torture, we get up from the table, and I tell Daddy that we must go and check into the house that he's rented for us and Paul, Elsie, and their kids to share that weekend.

We leave the apartment in silence. Scott wraps his arm around my waist and pulls me to him. As we walk back to the car, he turns to me and asks, "What the hell is one-pan lasagna?"

July 1983
Escondido, California

My Dear Daughter,

Thanks for your invite to spend some time with you. Just what I need. My arthritis can't cope with mother's behavior as she travels the same route to the hospital. Physically, I'm nigh depleted. I need that extra something. Thanks for your prayers.

For me to leave Sophie in her disturbed state may not be wise since she is now so detached from reality with no awareness at all of the needs of the household. Bluntly--she needs constant nursing care. Shows no responsibility.

Before you get this letter, I'll call and give you some details. My grief is that her behavior has detracted from my desires and plans for your wedding. It means so much to me that it will be a time of great happiness for you both. Towards that end, the enclosed "Tips on Marriage" is very sound advice. Read it with understanding and then keep on file for reference.

I'll call you between now and this letter's delivery. Thinking of you is my source of Joy.

Say hello to Scott.
I love you both.

Dad

August 1983

Scott and I are having so much fun planning our November wedding. There's nothing better than having our love for each other as an excuse to unite all the people in our diverse lives. Since Scott has one more year of college left, which includes the spring semester of his student teaching in Fort Worth, in the months before we marry, we look for a rental house in Northwest Dallas where we can begin our lives together. While still living in my efficiency, one morning I open the newspaper and look for what is available to rent on the west side of town. It doesn't take me long to see that a 3/2 house on Highgrove Drive is available for $475 a month—a great price as nothing else is available for under $500.

I dial the phone number and decide to only use my name, Christine Nicolette, as the person who is interested in the rental; from my past experience, I'm concerned that if I use my future last name and Scott's last name, Gonzalez, I may be speaking to a homeowner who might make inaccurate assumptions about us.

A man's voice answers my call, and I tell him that I'm a teacher and will soon be marrying another teacher. We are interested in renting this home and promise that we'll take very good care of it. His response is warm and affirming.

"My mom was a teacher for many years. I know she would love to know that two teachers are renting her home. Can you meet me there this afternoon?"

I wasn't expecting such a quick response. I tell him that my fiancé won't be available, but I will be. It would be best if I can rent it by myself without dealing with any type of possible prejudice on his part.

It works. This house appears to be the perfect place for us to have as our first home. I love the bright rooms and large, fenced backyard; maybe we can even get a dog! And the location is central to so much of what we do.

Out of deference to both of our parents, Scott and I decide not to live together until we are married. Since we both have come from conservative backgrounds, not just our parents, but also most of the people we know would label our living together as "living in sin." So, every weekend when Scott returns to Dallas from Denton, late each Friday and Saturday night he drives the twenty miles back to his mother's house to sleep.

But even without living together, we still have so much fun fixing up our future home. From buying a couch, to two bar stools, to a washer and dryer, to a queen-sized bed and more, we soon have established our cozy first home. And we know that in just a few months, we'll get to make it official; we can finally enjoy sleepovers every night.

November 1983 to April 1986

Thankfully, Mother is soon hospitalized again in California. I beg Daddy to not let her be released until after our November wedding. I already have started to have nightmares about her standing up in the middle of our vows and lifting her dress to expose herself as she urinates on the red church carpet. Thankfully, he seems to understand my fear and promises me that no matter what, she won't be there.

While she is in California's psychiatric hospitals, doctors have begun to give Mother a new drug called lithium. She is now diagnosed with severe neurosis and a bi-polar disorder. But unfortunately, while the medication seems to help her when she takes it, like most people with a mental illness, not one medical professional has ever been able to figure out how to ensure she will consistently take it.

On November 19, 1983, Scott and I delight in our beautiful and meaningful wedding ceremony at his family's church, Primera Iglesia Bautista, with a reception afterwards at a local hotel. Due to the respect that we have for our conservative parents and to avoid "rocking the boat," we decide that alcohol and dancing won't be part of the celebration. There is a poignant symmetry in the fact that we each have only one parent at our wedding.

We spend a relaxing Thanksgiving week honeymooning on the sunny beaches of Puerto Vallarta, Mexico, and then we return to Dallas to begin our new life together as husband and wife. In his wedding vows, Scott had said, "My family is now you." I finally know what it's like to live with a loyal foundation of strength and support. With Scott's love and my mother nowhere in sight, there is seemingly no height that is too high for me to fly.

And fly I do. I continue to have success developing an AP English program and helping an under-represented population of students have the opportunity to attend college.

Within a few years, I find more joy from creating a new family when I give birth to David Soames on December 14, 1985. Despite feeling totally unprepared for the tremendous life changes that motherhood brings, with Scott at my side, I feel like I'm part of a team that can face just about anything successfully.

After David is born, I miss having Daddy in my life even more. I try to convince him to move to Dallas. With his painful and worsening rheumatoid arthritis, there's only so much golf that he can play in Southern California, and as he's now close to eighty, he sure isn't getting younger. He needs to be with his family and not bear the incomprehensible weight of dealing with Mother by himself.

In between her hospital stays, Daddy finally tells Mother that he wants to be closer to at least one of his grandchildren. It's bad enough that he hasn't gotten to see Paul's two exceptional children, Tim and Sara, grow up; he must at least see ours. With him in the driver's seat, there is little she could do about her wish to remain living in what she has called "the perfect climate."

Daddy and Mother arrive in Dallas in April of 1986. Within a few months of their arrival, the nasty cycle begins, and Mother is once again thrown into the world of witchcraft and demons.

By now she has been treated in psychiatric hospitals in Long Island, New York; Wheaton, Illinois; Escondido, California; and Jerusalem, Israel. All that is left to complete the cycle of her being institutionalized wherever she lives is for her to be admitted to a hospital in Texas...and Terrell State Hospital it is.

December 1987
30 years old

I want to be a pansy
that stands tall and bright
ready for any gust of wind
or change of weather
never whining or sorrowful.

I want to be a pansy
and keep my flow and color
no matter what is around me
willing to mingle with
the rough bark of a tree
or with others who are different
and still know who I am.

I want to be a pansy
When the temperature drops
and water is sparse
when everything withers away
I want to be the one who
keeps hoping
keeps striving
keeps believing
in what could be.

I want to be a pansy
I want to slowly lift my head
and hear the sweet music of the day
and know
that the rough journey
has made me even stronger
than I was before.

May 1988

"Mommy, where's my teddy bear?"

I had been holding in my emotions for almost twenty-four hours; I couldn't hold them in any longer. I burst into tears and quickly walked out of David's bedroom.

It was yesterday when we were violated.

When I came home from work, I didn't find my childhood house gone mad, but the new home that Scott and I had so carefully crafted.

I walked into the kitchen, and the microwave was no longer sitting in its cart. In the living room, our china cabinet was open, and our china and crystal were missing.

I followed the evil tracks throughout our home. In every room were missing pieces. Scott's violin. The stereo and Bose speakers. Our ironing board and iron. Our new silverware. The Macintosh computer. A jade horse Scott's mom had brought back from China. All my priceless jewelry, including the wedding ring we had designed, but I couldn't wear due to my pregnancy swell. Scott's father's watch. Even my silk pajamas. And so much more.

But I didn't expect that the burglar would have slipped so low as to steal David's favorite teddy bear. It was enough that he had stolen the fireman sheets on his bed.

Someone with a child was setting up his house. How could a father be this evil?

I would not let evil win. Rather than run from it, I would face it and win. I wiped my tears, blew my nose, and walked back into David's bedroom. I joined him on his bed and wrapped my arm around him.

"David, I'm so sorry that your favorite teddy bear is gone. Most people are good, but there are a few people in this world who are bad because they've never learned to be good. While a bad man took a lot of our things, we still have each other. And nobody can ever take away the love that you and me and your daddy have for each other. That love is what makes our house into a home, and it's more important than anything we will ever buy."

October 1988 to December 1988

Our final family birth miracle occurs on October 10, 1988 when our daughter Analise Nicole is born. Surprisingly, at the time of my daughter's birth, Mother has been out of Terrell State Hospital for a few months and is still relatively well. After missing every other major milestone in my life, my mother is at the hospital a few hours after my daughter's birth. By her kind words and behavior, it's obvious that she and Daddy relish the idea that like them, Scott and I and Paul and Elsie now have both an older son and a younger daughter.

Three days after Analise's birth, Scott and David arrive to pick us up at the Mesquite Community Hospital. We are finally the complete family of four that I've always dreamed of having. After carefully strapping both of our children in, Scott starts our maroon Honda Accord and begins the short drive home. As he drives, I feel a few tears on my cheeks. I reach for his hand and silently vow to be the mother that I always wished I had when I was growing up.

Just a few weeks after Analise's birth, after working on it for several years, I finally complete writing my master's thesis, a casebook called *Teaching Hermann Hesse as a Contemporary Pilgrim*. On the December night when I learn that my long thesis has been approved by my three-member committee, and I've finally earned my master's degree in the humanities, I feel so empowered.

If I was able to do this while juggling all that is on my plate each day, there is probably no limit to what I can do with my life.

Now it's Scott's turn to further his education, so in his limited free time from parenting small children and teaching English, on Saturdays, evenings, and during the summer, he begins to attend classes so he can eventually earn a master's degree in humanities from The University of Dallas.

We've now entered the most challenging years of our lives. We're trying our best to balance our all-consuming jobs as English teachers with raising two small children—and we must also find time to care for my aging parents. But having Daddy nearby is the right thing to do, albeit the tough thing. I'm relieved just knowing that he isn't so far away and that he doesn't have to deal with Mother's erratic mental illness by himself.

January 1989
31 years old

I felt a deep tenderness for Mother yesterday—a feeling I've never felt for her before. It was her seventy-third birthday. As usual, she wanted nothing. I never have been able to give her anything. The few times I've attempted to add to the nothing she has, it didn't fit, she didn't like it, or she had no use for it. "Keep the money. You need it so much for yourself."

Our lives have been so different. I have thousands of dollars more than she had at my age, a beautiful new house with fine furniture, brand new appliances and drapes, two cars—even a garage door opener! Scott and I have enjoyed six happy years together, and now we have a son and a daughter. I work for a living and love my career. She stopped working many years before she had children. She is a loner; I am a people person. She never graduated from high school; I have earned my graduate degree. She is sedentary; I am active. She lives for heaven; I live for earth. I smile and shine like Daddy; she is a parasite living off Daddy's and my happiness. She has been so sick; I try to live beyond her sickness. Yet sometimes I still feel love for her. She asks for so little from life. The few times when she isn't sick, she lives for her husband and children. She cares for nothing material from this earth—such a rare value, especially in Dallas. During my life I have been ashamed of her more times than I can count. Yesterday, I was proud of her in a way I have never been before.

March 1989

Since his late twenties, my brother Paul has resided close to his wife's family dairy farm in southern New Jersey. Despite the distance between us, Paul and Elsie and their two kids venture to Dallas to visit Daddy and Mother once a year—usually at Thanksgiving.

We both have been blessed to marry into situations where our spouse's large family is nearby; consequently, our children have been raised around their grandparents, aunts, uncles, and cousins. And now with Daddy's advanced age and his inability to travel to see them, Paul occasionally makes the trip to Dallas alone to visit with his parents for a few days.

I always enjoy seeing Paul, perhaps primarily because of the special bond we shared when we grew up in our madhouse of a family. We both learned to escape from our mother's demonic antics in different ways—me, by running from them, and Paul, by immersing himself in magazines and books.

Since his childhood, he's read incessantly and has also been fascinated by computers. Later, after attending his high school classes at Stony Brook School for Boys, he could cross the train tracks to enter Stony Brook University where he would play at programming a computer that filled a huge, glass-walled room. Often, he would enter a Radio Shack and seemingly get lost in it; it always took several strong attempts to get him out.

It was relating to people that was always more challenging for Paul than it was for me. But when it came down to it, few had a kinder and more generous heart than my brother.

He bought me a "Chris, Sweetest 16" charm for my charm bracelet, brought me back a gorgeous pearl broach from his summer spent in Japan, sent me my first flowers for my seventeenth birthday, bought me a shiny, new Schwinn bicycle before I left for college, and then gave me his car as my first car.

In 1978, he wisely married Elsie, a competent and understanding woman who has patiently helped him learn to live a more balanced life.

This week is one of the times that Paul is coming to Dallas by himself. Mother is still hospitalized at Terrell; it will be nice to have Paul visit her so I won't have to. How I hate giving up hours of my precious free time with David and Analise on Sunday afternoons to venture thirty-five miles east to a ghost-like town and buildings with halls that smell like they have been scrubbed for centuries without success.

And then there is the reality of seeing Mother. I never know what condition she will be in or if she will even want to see me. Several times I've made the long trip early in her treatment, and she has refused to come out of her room. But when she agrees to see me, I watch as she shuffles down the hallway looking as disheveled and drugged as they always have her, with drool ceaselessly dripping down her hair-stubbled chin.

We're always directed to a small, almost empty waiting area where we sit on two hard, black wood chairs and pretend to be interested in each other. I attempt to make small talk with her for about thirty minutes as I mostly fill her in on how David and Analise are doing. She usually replies with just a word or two. In the past, I've been described as someone who can talk to anyone easily, but when I visit my mother in this dreadful place, there is never enough to talk about.

I know that as her daughter I must continue to make these trips to see her—if for no other reason than because it is the right thing to do. Recently, my theology has added the element of karma to its tenets; who knows when I will need someone to visit me in my advanced years?

Paul is due back from Terrell at 4:00 p.m., and it's almost 5:00 p.m., and we still haven't heard anything from him. It gets to be 5:30 p.m., and since we had told him we would be eating an early dinner together, we're concerned that something bad could have happened to him. Scott tells me he'll get in the car and start driving slowly toward Terrell to see if Paul had car trouble in our Honda. Less than five minutes later, Scott returns to the house with an angry look on his face.

"You won't believe where I found him. He was parked at the end of our block sitting in our car reading a magazine."

April 1989

What is the worst thing you've ever done? I sure don't have a tough time deciding what mine is, because I did it this morning.

Since Mother is still in the hospital, and Daddy is spending so much time by himself, this Sunday morning we invited him to join us at Primera Iglesia Bautista. When we pulled up to the church, I got out of the backseat and came around to let Daddy out of the front seat. Then the arduous process of his getting out of our car began. As I opened his car door, he slowly raised his painful legs up and swung them around. Next, as he braced his right hand on the column between the front and back doors, he lifted himself up. While he was doing this, I was getting David out of the back seat, and Scott was unstrapping Analise from her car seat.

Thinking Daddy was completely out of the car, I closed the front door of the car and heard an unfamiliar and sickening crunch.

Suddenly, we heard Daddy cry out in a sound of loud guttural pain unlike any I had ever heard before.

I had closed the door of the car on his right pinky!

Scott and I rushed to him and saw that the top half of his little finger was hanging from the bone.

Scott quickly took off his shirt, wrapped it around Daddy's finger, told him to keep pressure on it to hold it together, and helped him back into our car. Somehow, I got the kids back in the car, and we set off for the hospital ER.

If anyone didn't need to feel more pain, it was my daddy. All his years enduring Mother's mental illness, all his years in debilitating pain from his arthritis, and now I did this. Thankfully, the doctor was able insert a pin into the bone and to sew his pinky back together, but when we left Daddy at his apartment, he was still in a lot of pain.

I must have said "I'm sorry" over a hundred times, but it sure wasn't good enough; my words didn't take Daddy's pain away.

Each time I apologized, Daddy, with his hand wrapped and elevated and with his eyes closed, kept repeating, "It's okay, Christine. I know that it was an accident, and accidents happen."

Yes, I know this. But how could I ever forgive myself for hurting this man whom I love so much and who has loved me longer and harder than anyone else in the world?

My tribute to my wife Sophie, addressed to our children Paul and Christine:

Today, June 24, 1989, marks my eighty-second birthday.

In the absence of Sophie, who is presently hospitalized, my daughter has planned an occasion to celebrate since it is the day which we were both born. My son Paul will be here with his family, too. My regret is that my wife and my children's mother, Sophie, is unable to attend.

Why do I miss her presence? Here's why. In the twilight of my life, I ponder who this wife of mine and mother of my children really is. As I make my visits to the hospital and fellowship with her, this is what I see:

This girl turned three years of casual companionship into a situation of great love when unbeknownst to me, she became a "new creation" in Christ. This "new creation" stumped me, for immediately her former worldly activities of theatre-going, smoking, and pleasure-bound pursuits became of no importance. She cleaned up her act so much that to my amazement, shy, demure Sophie stood before a gathering of hundreds of nurses, patients, and doctors at the Norwegian Hospital in Brooklyn and delivered a most convincing, powerful testimony on what accepting Jesus Christ as personal Savior meant in her life. Her performance and convincing delivery settled it for skeptical Charles. She was the one I loved, and I must have her as my wife. We became man and wife on February 7th, 1942, 47 years ago.

This is a capsule of her love and devotion to me during our early years together:

1942--We married at the American Seminary of the Bible, where she became a student when I was inducted in the 76th Army Division in Ft. Meade, Maryland. She followed me to Ft. Meade where she rented a room in the home of the warden of the Maryland Jessup Penitentiary, and she took care of the needs of her $50-a-month-buck-private husband by finding a job and supporting me as I went through basic training. She was my spiritual strength, and God blessed our weekend get-togethers.

1943--This was a year of the mighty display of God's hand in our lives. Sophie assuaged the agonizing pain I had after a faulty hemorrhoidectomy by covertly entering my ward to comfort me for hours at length. Her loving attention was a boon to speed my healing.

Then as the wife of a mere Buck Private, she miraculously gained admission to Walter Reed Hospital's ward for wives of officers for her thyroglossal cyst operation by the best plastic surgeon in the southwest, Major Schussler. I still can't believe my holy boldness to visit her three or four times from Ft. Mead in my GI uniform!

May 1943--As officer material, I was sent to Camp Barkeley in Texas to become a ninety-day officer. At age 36, I wasn't too enthusiastic, since I had to compete with men 10-15 years my junior. After failing test #1, who was the person that arrived as an angel to hold me up to cope with the rigorous teaching and training? Your mother. At that time, to come to Abilene from Brooklyn was to travel for days in a coach crowded with soldiers who were crisscrossing the country. I sure appreciated her dogged spirit in her effort to be with me.

While I was trying to cope with the high-pressure program to emerge as an officer of the United States Army, what was Sophie's involvement? Along with taking care of my personal attire--washing, pressing my uniforms, and meal preparation on weekend leaves in our room in Abilene--as a Jewess who had accepted Christ as her Savior, she was a rarity in Texas and was invited to give her personal testimony in many churches and on local radio stations. Her exemplary Christian testimony brought blessings to many.

August 1943--I received my 2nd lieutenant gold bar, and with Sophie's experiences as a wise shopper, I became the best-dressed 36-year-old soldier in Texas. My first assignment was as a Medical Admissions Officer at Brooks General Hospital in San Antonio. My five-month stay there with my Sophie was a taste in luxury living, as we lived in the home of retired county Judge Edwards. God dealt with us munificently. We visited the First Baptist Church in town and had the warmest of fellowships.

1944-1946--Sophie followed me to San Francisco where I was Quartermaster Supply Officer and spent a month at Fort Mason in the shadow of the Golden Gate Bridge making certain that the 718 Medical Company would have all the equipment necessary to bring Japan to her knees. Through it all, Sophie shared a guest house room at the Fort. When our company boarded ship and headed to the Solomon Islands, there was Sophie faithfully present to bid me a fond farewell as we embraced with a prayer.

From the day she received my APO address from overseas, she never missed a day in sending me a four-page letter that proved my daily spiritual shot-in-the-arm. I've saved many of those letters, and I intend to have you share them as memorabilia of the love that was your mother and dad's beginning.

So please deal lovingly and kindly with your Mother for contributing so much in bringing out some of the good things that I may have demonstrated. May God bless you as He did us through the years.

Your loving Dad

December 1989

It is so tough to see Daddy this frail. The arthritis that has plagued him throughout the past twelve years has progressed to such a point that he struggles to take each step. Just getting up from a chair is now so painful for him. Thankfully, I bought him a self-rising recliner several years ago; without it, I'm not sure how he would function each day. Mother is still in Terrell State Hospital, thankfully, but this also means that Daddy is living alone--something I hate.

Daddy fills his days by driving to get a copy of *The Dallas Times Herald* and a cinnamon cake donut and coffee at Dunkin' Donuts each morning. There he completes the challenging crossword puzzle in the few minutes that it takes him to eat the donut and drink his coffee. Most afternoons he makes the long drive out to Terrell to visit Mother. He also has created a putting green in his apartment that he made from cutting a Kleenex box in half. In his small living room, he loves practicing putting golf balls into the box. I call him daily to check on him, but that still doesn't seem like enough. But with the prospect of mother coming home from the hospital yet again, there are clearly no alternatives to his living arrangement.

How we love Saturday mornings! That's the time Daddy comes over for his weekly breakfast visits. He usually uses the Grandy's or McDonald's drive-thrus to pick up breakfast for all of us--biscuit and egg sandwiches for me and Scott, and pancakes and sausage for the kids; he eats the leftovers and drinks his beloved coffee. He has told us his favorite time each week is when he gets to see David, who is about to turn four, and Analise, who is a little over a year old now. And we have quickly learned that this is one of the best win-wins. Due to

Scott's father's tragic suicide, Daddy will be the only grandfather our children will ever know.

I look out the living room window of our two-story home and see his light green Buick coming slowly around our cul-de-sac.

"David! Analise! Come downstairs. Grandpa is here!"

I hear them scramble from their room. How they love seeing their grandpa!

As Daddy pulls up in front of our house, I slip on a jacket and head outside to greet him. When I get to his car, I see him reach into the Styrofoam cup that he keeps in the front console. In it he stores all the change that he finds and spare change that he gets back from his cash transactions; each Saturday he brings in the change along with breakfast. He knows that I'll save it, eventually roll it, and then deposit half of it in each of the kids' college accounts.

"Good Morning, Daddy!"

"Heelloo," he says with a grin on his face.

"Let me help you." I loop the plastic bag over my left arm and reach out with my right hand as he takes it and uses it for support to get out of the car. Then he reaches in the back seat for his two canes, one silver and one black, that will help him walk. I notice that his blue shirt is still heavily stained with coffee spills, and his tan pants look like they haven't been washed in months.

With his arm linked to mine, we walk more slowly than usual up to my home. He seems to be in pain; it must be the cold weather.

David and Analise are waiting inside our home and are clearly happy to see him--David is literally jumping around already. Analise keeps saying, "Pancake! Pancake!" We used to think that word was for the pancakes that he brings, but we recently realized that her name for her grandfather is now "Pancake."

We head to the kitchen table and unfold the breakfast treasures that he has bought for the five of us. After saying a prayer and enjoying our breakfast together, it's time for Daddy to read to the kids in the special rocker we bought him last year that isn't too hard for him to lower his body into. Scott brings over some new books we've been saving for today, and then the fun begins. Clearly, one of Daddy's favorite things to do is to read to his grandchildren.

Scott knows what to do next. He hasn't clipped Daddy's tough toenails for a few months—something that Daddy hasn't been able to do for himself for years—so Scott asks Daddy if today is a good day to clip them. Daddy quickly acquiesces and slips off his woven loafers. How dry the skin on his legs is! His toenails now resemble long claws. I watch as Scott slowly and lovingly cuts each nail, making sure that each broken piece is carefully put aside before he moves on to the next nail. If my daddy ever questioned whether I married the right person, I know that every doubt has long been removed.

After a couple of hours at our house, Daddy says that he must leave and make the trip to Terrell to visit Mother.

"Can you come along with me to visit her today?"

"Sorry, Daddy. I don't have time because all afternoon I'll be in a graduate class. Remember I told you I'm taking it so I can be endorsed to teach the gifted?"

"That's right. Well do take care of yourself, Christine. I think you are doing too much right now."

Scott, David, and Analise join me as we slowly walk Daddy back to his car, help him get inside, and wave as he slowly drives off.

Today, he didn't seem as upbeat as he usually is. I suspect that he is in a great deal of pain.

April 1990

It's a bright Saturday morning, and Scott and I are fluttering around the house preparing for a wedding—yes, a wedding—that will take place in our home at 4:00 p.m. this afternoon. I had offered to host a wedding shower for my good friend and colleague Jan, but a few days ago, she called and asked if it could be changed to a wedding instead, since all the people who would be invited to her wedding—her second—would be attending the shower. Just. Wow. But how can we say no?

Thankfully, we decided this was a good day to bring the kids to *Abuela's*, Scott's mother's, home. She lives just a few miles away, and she had recently been asking repeatedly to see them. As Scott begins to vacuum the carpet, I hear the phone ring.

"Hello?"

"Christine. This is your dad. I need your help, please. I have a doctor appointment at 9:00 a.m. this morning, and I was wondering if you can pick me up and take me to it. Something isn't right."

"*What?* What's wrong, Daddy?" My heart begins to beat faster.

"I'm not sure. I'll know more after I see the doctor."

"Of course. Give me fifteen minutes, okay?" Daddy has never asked me for help before. It doesn't matter what is happening at our house later that afternoon. I hang up and ask Scott to turn the vacuum off. I tell him about the call.

"Don't worry about a thing, Christine. You need to be with him. I'll finish cleaning the house and get the food ready. We have plenty of time."

How I love this man.

Fifteen minutes later, I swing by Daddy's apartment, and he's standing outside waiting for me on his porch. Once he gets into my car, I notice that the coloring on his face looks very odd. Didn't I just see him last week?

"I need for you to drive me to see my doctor, Dr. Rothstein. It's not too far from here."

"Don't worry, Daddy. What's wrong?"

"When I urinated this morning, the liquid that came out was a dark brown. Since I've been experiencing some upper-gastro pain for quite a while, I think it's time to get this situation checked out."

We arrive at Dr. Rothstein's office, and I breathe a sigh of relief. How great it is that this doctor is open for half a day on Saturdays!

Dr. Rothstein has been waiting for him. Daddy asks me to remain in the waiting area because he will probably be getting a complete physical. I take a seat and begin to pray.

About fifteen minutes later, Daddy comes back to the reception area with the doctor at his side.

He introduces me to Dr. Rothstein.

"Your father has something seriously wrong with him that I'm unable to help. But I have already called my friend who is a doctor at Baylor Hospital, and he'll be waiting for you when you arrive there."

I feel like a tidal wave has hit me. I ask to use the office phone to call Scott. After a few rings, Scott answers, and as I tell him about Daddy's situation, I can feel a lump forming in my throat and tears filling my eyes. I can barely get the news out.

Scott tells me to calm down. Everything is going to be okay. But I need to be with Daddy right now. Everything is under control at our house; in fact, it's just about cleaned—just the downstairs guest bathroom is left. We hang up. Once again, Scott is the best point-person imaginable in a difficult situation.

About thirty-minutes later, we arrive at Baylor Hospital in East Dallas. I take a parking ticket and accompany Daddy to the Emergency Room where Dr. Rothstein has told us to go first. Amazingly, the woman at the front desk is expecting us, so despite an overflowing crowd in the reception area, Daddy is quickly taken back to a room.

While we wait for the doctor, Daddy tells me how much he loves me and appreciates my being with him right now. No matter what the diagnosis is, he promises to do his best to cure himself of it—even if it means flying to Mayo Clinic and being seen by the best doctors in the world. Because of the joy he derives from his children's growing families, he knows he has so much to live for. And then he tells me that he knows that his situation right now is a pay-back for all the sweets that he has given into throughout his life; how he has always loved his donuts and apple pie!

Daddy has always been a lean machine. Unlike my mother and me, he and my brother have metabolisms that quickly process everything they eat. If Daddy has overindulged in sweets, I sure haven't seen him do it or seen any extra weight that normally comes when someone overindulges. But he's always been so weight conscious, and like my mother, food is a constant topic of conversation.

During the next few hours, Daddy is taken in and out of the room as a variety of medical procedures are done. Several times, I ask to use the phone at the nurse's station and check in with Scott. It's already 1:00 p.m.—the wedding is still on, and everything is ready. Bless him.

At 1:30 p.m., Daddy is back again in the room, and with him is Dr. Hakert, whom he has been referred to see. Dr. Hakert introduces himself and then asks me to sit down. He tells me that the tests revealed that Daddy has a very virulent cancerous tumor in his gallbladder, and the cancerous cells have already spread to his bile duct. That is why Daddy's skin color and the whites of his eyes are so yellow—his bile duct is blocked by the tumor, too.

I sit there in disbelief. Daddy's eyes begin to water. Mine join in.

"Can anything be done?" I ask.

"It's too late for anything to be done. At his advanced age of eighty-two, it probably is best for him to be kept as comfortable as possible. With the cases that I've seen like his, the average life expectancy is eight weeks."

We sit there in silence trying to absorb the words we've just heard. We learn that the "good news" is that because his cancer is terminal, Daddy will easily qualify for hospice care, and this service will help keep him out of pain for as long as possible. Then Dr. Hakert tells us how sorry he is about the situation.

"What foods should I eat now?" Daddy asks.

"Anything you want," Dr. Hakert responds.

Dr. Hakert hands us information on hospice care and tells Daddy that he wants to see him in a couple of weeks to check in with how he is doing.

Daddy and I leave the hospital in silence.

My worst nightmare has just occurred. I always dreaded that with a father who was fifty when I was born, I would be called to the school office one day and be told that my daddy had died in one way or another. I was so fearful of losing him—not only because he was the person whom I loved the most and who loved me the most but also because it would mean that I would be left to be the caregiver and decision maker for my mother—the mother I could still barely stand to be around.

As I was growing up, I'd often tell Daddy that he must live not only to see me get married, but also, he must live long enough to hold both my son and my daughter, and I was hoping to have a son first. The fear of his quick passing has now come to fruition, but much later than I ever thought it would. And he has lived long enough to meet my husband and to hold both my son and daughter. For this I am so grateful.

I drop Daddy off at his apartment. Never has my goodbye kiss on his cheek been more poignant. We hug in silence. He slowly gets out of the car, and I watch as he uses his two crutches to walk into his apartment. I tell him I'll call him in a few hours.

By the time I arrive home, it is 3:00 p.m. Scott meets me at the door, and as the tears flow, I tell him Daddy's prognosis. He holds me tight. I never want to leave his arms, but I know I must. I head upstairs to change into clothes for the wedding.

May 1990

Life always brings the yin with the yang. In the middle of the final weeks of Daddy's life, I'm also facing the most important night of my professional life. This year, in addition to teaching AP English, I'm using my graduate training in talented and gifted education to begin and direct a program for the creatively gifted students at North Dallas High School. It has been so gratifying to work with these students as many of them have never been recognized for their intelligence. And due to their impoverished family backgrounds, limited English proficiency, or both, they don't believe in what they could grow to be. I sure believe in them.

The program espouses the philosophy of giftedness by the renowned theorist Dr. Joseph Renzulli. His concept of giftedness is comprised of three elements: above average intelligence, creativity, and task commitment. My charge has been to develop an identification tool for my students, many of whom are from other countries and have only lived in the United States for a few years, and then to create an interdisciplinary curriculum that focuses on developing each of their strengths. For the past year, we have been studying the themes of conflict and patterns; this fall, Jane Goodall, the famous primatologist, will visit our school, so I am already working on developing curriculum for the theme of conservation.

Now that it's the end of the first year of the program, each of my students has created a project that focuses on his or her strengths and builds on what was learned this year. Their projects will be showcased in a special event called Laureate in the Limelight. Since my school is piloting this program, and we have received quite a bit of media coverage, I feel the pressure to showcase both my and my students' work accurately and well. Tonight, May 10th, is the night of this event, and the theorist himself, Dr. Renzulli, will be here from Connecticut to see the program and my students' work.

I don't have time to go home after school today as there is still too much to do. I have to make sure the student projects are beautifully displayed in the school cafeteria, the refreshments are organized and ready to go, my room is set up with a creative and accurate display of the two interdisciplinary themes, and the nametags and programs that the students created are ready to be distributed to our guests.

By 6:15 p.m., all thirty-eight of my students have assembled in the school auditorium where the program will be introduced, and their excitement is palpable. I see several of their parents already sitting in their seats. In the background, I hear Regoberto Cortez practicing his original rap that will introduce the program. He will also provide original music later in the evening.

"Can I go to the classroom and make sure all the sound equipment is ready for my duet with Dulce?" Willy Flores asks.

"Of course. While you're there, please do a final check to make sure everything's ready to go." Even though Willy is a freshman, he is one of my most responsible students.

I feel Cynthia Villasenor's arm around my shoulder. Cynthia is my writer, and she has written a captivating novella and then constructed a jukebox that complements her story. She has been one of my neediest students this year but also one with great talent. I reach to hug her back.

"You're going to do a great job tonight, Cynthia. I'm so proud of your hard work."

I see Nhu Phang and Keang Pol huddled together in a corner of the auditorium and walk up to them: "Are you ready to show off your great work?"

"We so nervous. We don't speak English very good."

"Don't worry. Just be yourselves and show your projects to everyone who walks by. Your great work will speak for itself."

At 7:00 p.m. the school auditorium is already quite full. I look around and see a few faces of professionally dressed people whom I don't recognize. Scott and his mom are there to support me, and even several of my good friends have arrived. Then I see Dr. Emily Stewart, the district director of the program, surrounded by other important-looking people, one of whom must be Dr. Renzulli.

My principal, Oscar Rodriquez, begins the night by welcoming everyone and telling them how pleased he is to have had this program at his school. Then he introduces me. I can feel my heart beating as I walk to the podium and begin my short introduction.

Three hours later, I arrive back home totally fulfilled but also exhausted. I couldn't be happier about how the night went or prouder of each of my kids as they confidently explained their projects. I make my way up the stairs and crack open the door to peek my head into the bedroom that David and Analise share. They are sleeping soundly; they must have had so much fun tonight with their babysitter, Yarid. Scott is already in bed and is waiting for me.

"Congratulations, baby. You did such a great job."

"Thanks for being there to support me. I was so proud of my kids. Did you see even shy Dora smiling as she explained her paintings on the Holocaust? I couldn't believe it when Dr. Renzulli told me afterwards that he has never seen an inner-city talented and gifted program at this level. I can't wait to tell the kids how impressed he was by their work."

A few minutes later I get into bed. I think about how many parents spend much of their time and money trying to help their children improve their weaknesses. Tonight, I learned what happens when you focus on finding and developing their strengths. I hope that as David and Analise grow, I'll always remember to do this.

June 24th, 1990

The day has come—our last birthday to share. It will be Daddy's eighty-third and my thirty-third. Throughout my life it always has been so special to share my birthday with my daddy, my birthday twin; sharing a birthday with him added to the special connection that we've always had. I don't know when Daddy will be gone, but one thing is clear: he sure won't be celebrating another birthday with me. He has already lived three weeks beyond the doctor's eight-week estimate. He's already lost quite a few pounds since his diagnosis, and due to his increased weakness, it's even harder for him to get around.

But he is still alive, and we will celebrate today. I know that apple pie à la mode is his favorite dessert, but we've just returned from our annual trip to Ham Orchards in Terrell, one of our favorite places to buy the sweetest peaches we've ever tasted, so he tells me that a peach pie sounds even better. Scott is a better pie maker than I and offers to make Daddy a pie from scratch. Paul has flown in from New Jersey for our afternoon get-together.

I am thirty-three today, the age Jesus was when he was crucified, and seeing my beloved daddy die this slow and painful death feels like a type of crucifixion. Daddy doesn't deserve this level of pain—especially after experiencing so much of it throughout his life when dealing with my mother.

Miraculously, Mother is still well, and I've never seen her be this kind to Daddy. Perhaps being his legs as she brings him the many glasses of water he asks for each day and helping him get around their apartment is giving her a renewed sense of purpose. I wonder if she realizes that if she thought she was screwed by his demons while he was alive, she's really going to be screwed when he dies and she is alone, mostly left to fend for herself. Who will have the unconditional love for her that he had?

Daddy and Mother will arrive at 2:00 p.m. Paul is still upstairs reading, and David and Analise have been playing in the den all morning. David has been playing lots of Nintendo these days, and I'm glad he has that escape as I have spent so much time with Daddy and have been crying on and off throughout each day. At four months shy of five years old, David is old enough to recognize my sadness, and he doesn't need to. At twenty months, thankfully, Analise doesn't have a clue.

I must be strong for Daddy. I must remember that death is a part of life, and each of us will one day die. And I must remain grateful for the thirty-three years that I have had him in my life—many more years than I ever imagined.

August 1990
Age 33

It doesn't matter
that you were eighty-three
feeble, arthritic, in agony
and prepared.
You were too
young to die.
I can never replace the
Saturday mornings,
the crossword puzzles,
your smile
and encouragement.
You were my fan club.
Your life brightened my life.
You loved my family and
they loved you back.
You weren't really
prepared
to die
were you?
You fought to the end, unwilling
to yield to the Victor.
In four days of unstoppable rain
like Christ on the cross
you were in agony, thirsty,
aware of your pain.
"It is contingent on me"
You were too young to die.
I will never understand death, even
with the prospect of eternal life.
Why the suffering?

Why the absence?
I know I will carry you in me
but that is not enough,
You were too young to die.
Come on...
pull around the corner
once again in that
green luxurious car of yours.
Open the car door ever so slowly.
Strain to wiggle those toes past the brakes.
Feel the pain. Cringe in your mouth.
Move your legs slowly around the brakes.
Struggle to get up.
Analise is waiting for her Pancake.
The pain is worth it all, Daddy.
You were too young to die.

October 1991
Age 34

Gifts from Hell

I blamed you for the
2659 hellmiles
we drove from
Miami to San Diego
miles that sang
my impatience and fear,
and only one way out—
through my mouth.

But now I see
that you were the one
who gave me the drive
to travel life's rough miles
and carry optimism,
crossword puzzles,
and a deep faith
with me.

So what I thought was
a living hell
was simply just a workout
(of sorts)
so I thank you
for this
Daddy.

January 1992

The time to answer the million-dollar question has come: *What will I do with my mother?*

With my brother Paul living over 1,500 miles away, I'm now the only person responsible for her care in whatever type of facility I can find that will take her. After spending hours researching what facilities would accept a woman with her medical and mental history, Scott and I find a nursing center that is willing to admit her, but it's close to fifty miles east of Dallas in Quinlan, Texas. My plate is overly full raising two young children, directing talented and gifted programs at two middle schools, spending time with Scott, and making the 100-mile trip to visit my mother on Sunday afternoons.

Although my mother is still the greatest challenge in my life, many of my dreams have now come true.

In May, we find a two-story home in Sparkman Club, a cohesive neighborhood in Northwest Dallas—and a neighborhood that is fifteen miles closer to Greenhill School where Scott now teaches, and David has just completed kindergarten. After we move in, we learn that Analise has also been accepted into Greenhill's preschool, so now all three of my family members will attend this excellent educational institution each day. Since faculty members receive a substantial tuition reduction for their children, amazingly, we will pay a very nominal amount for our children's excellent education.

Then in June, I receive a phone call from the principal at my dream school—the highly acclaimed Booker T. Washington High School for the Performing and Visual Arts. Through one of my former administrators, Dr. Watkins has heard about my teaching success and wants me to consider working in a teaching position he has created for me; as usual, there is no turnover at the school.

After a quick phone interview, he tells me that I'm hired and to report to in-service in late August. I'm simply elated to have the opportunity to work at this school as I've heard so much about it and have always been passionate about the arts. It also seems like it will be the perfect setting for me to continue to be a catalyst for creativity in my classroom.

But with this newfound joy, I begin to have a recurring fear that something bad is going to happen to me.

The school year begins, and I'm assigned to teach three different types of classes—none that I have ever taught before. In total, I have 135 students in my classes. These students are radically different from those I've taught for the past thirteen years, as they come from predominantly middle-class families, have mostly strong educational backgrounds, and about half of them are Caucasian.

Quickly, I realize that I don't have enough time in the day to adequately prepare for three different types of English classes, to grade my students' quizzes and essays, and to take care of my home and family responsibilities. But nobody knows what this stress is doing inside my body because on the outside, I'm still my enthusiastic, happy, and seemingly accomplished self.

March 1992

As I suspected, getting consistent care for Mother is a tremendous burden. The administrators at the facility in Quinlan called a few weeks ago, and we learned that since Mother was so aggressive with the patients there, they are only going to be able to keep her till the end of March.

So, what do we do with her?

I continue to research places that may be able to take her. I talk to doctors at Terrell and at her Quinlan residence. Nobody seems to know any facility that will admit someone who not only needs geriatric care but also psychiatric care—and someone with a case history as extreme as my mother's. In addition to this, the only money that Mother has to pay for her care is her monthly Social Security checks and Medicaid, which we just learned she qualifies for.

Thankfully, Paul has flown down to Dallas to help us decide what to do with Mother next. I'm so glad that this time I won't have to make the decision about Mother's care by myself. After dinner, Scott and I meet with Paul to discuss our findings. He has done some research, too, and he feels that the few facilities we want to explore further are not acceptable for his mother.

His mother is a very different person than my mother.

Mother invested her firstborn dreams in Paul, so he was always the last to be accused of witchcraft. I was Daddy's girl; Paul was Mother's boy. He was nine, not five, when the manifestations of Mother's mental illness began, and he often was away at school or had locked himself in his bedroom to read while I dealt with the reality of our mother's behavior. As much as I love Paul, I am resentful that he is treating our obscene mother with his kid gloves.

After we listen to him for a while and try not to say anything that we'll later regret, Scott is unable to contain himself.

"You come down here on your white stallion, and you think that you know what to do and can change everything. And then you just leave. We are tired of this, Paul."

"It sounds to me like you both have given up hope," Paul responds.

"We haven't given up hope, Paul. We feel the way we do because for decades, we've dealt with the reality of your mother's illness. Because she continues to refuse to take the medication to keep her well and to control her mood swings, there are few facilities that are set up to deal with a person with her extreme behavior."

Miraculously, an administrator at Terrell State Hospital calls us a few days later and tells us about a facility that has just opened in far south Dallas that may be able to accommodate our mother—a psychiatric nursing home, one of the few of its kind, called Southaven Nursing Center. We must check it out.

April 1992

It's Wednesday night, and I've decided to move out of my small group comfort zone and for the first time to attend a Greenhill School parent book club meeting. One reason I decide to do this is because the book selection was written by one of my favorite writers and people, Madeleine L'Engle. As a child, I read *A Wrinkle in Time* countless times, and then years later I was blessed to hear her speak several times at Wheaton College. The book club selection is *Two-Part Invention: The Story of a Marriage*; the title alone sounds so appealing.

Then I learn it's the true story of how she dealt with the death of her beloved husband, the actor Hugh Franklin. I've always been a sucker for a poignant love story.

I don't know many Greenhill parents, so I enter the Montgomery Library tentatively, scanning the room for a familiar face. When I don't see one, I take a chair in the L-shaped back section of the room. A few minutes later, the room is filled, and the discussion begins.

The facilitator and librarian, Mrs. Baker, begins by asking what we thought about the book. Well, it sure resonated well with me. One of my favorite passages was, "If we accept that we have at least an iota of free will, we cannot throw it back the moment things go wrong. Like a human parent, God will help us when we ask for help, but in a way that will make us more mature, more real, not in a way that will diminish us. And God does not wave a magic wand and clean up the planet we have abused. Our polluted planet is causing more people to die of cancer than when the skies and seas and earth were clean."

How could I not love this read?

One at a time people begin to express their feelings about the book, and all of them are surprisingly negative. One person thinks the book is too melodramatic, another doesn't respect the writing, and another feels that its approach is too Christian to reach a large audience.

I feel like I can't just sit there without sharing my truth. I raise my hand tentatively. Mrs. Baker motions for me to speak.

"I thought this book was a courageous and insightful read about the highest form of love that two people can share. As I read it, I was reminded of what it means when you vow to love someone unconditionally in both sickness and in health. I also appreciated L'Engle's honesty when she wrote, 'The growth of love is not a straight line, but a series of hills and valleys.'"

I could hear my voice shaking.

Then I hear another voice, whose face I can't see because it's coming from the unseen part of the L-shaped room.

"I agree. I absolutely loved this book and learned so much about the power of love from it. I recently lost my brother to cancer, and so much of what she wrote about dealing with one of the most horrific experiences that a person can endure echoed my experience. Actually, this was one of the best books I've read in a really long time."

Who was this person talking? I must find her.

No other positive comments are made about the book, and I try to be patient and understand the other negative opinions that I hear. I'm totally thrown off guard by the negativity; clearly, these people want to intellectualize and criticize what they read more than feel it.

But I still must find the person who loved the book.

Afterwards, I make my way around the room, searching for a kind face. It doesn't take me long to bump into another person who looks like she is searching for someone, too.

"Are you the one who liked the book?" I hear her ask.

"Yes! Thanks for your great words about it; I didn't feel so alone. I'm Christine. What's your name?"

I learn that her name is Janis Dworkis, and amazingly, she also has a son, Michael, in the second grade. She tells me she is a freelance writer. Wow. Can it be that I've finally found a Greenhill parent who has a profession and interests that are closer to mine? Already, I see great depth and beauty coming from her eyes.

"Would you like to meet for coffee sometime so we can get to know each other better?" she asks.

"That would be wonderful."

I don't realize it then, but one of the most significant relationships in my life has just begun.

September 1992

I'm teaching my third-period English III class and am in the middle of a sentence about Ralph Waldo Emerson's "Self-Reliance," when I feel my heart skip a beat. Then another skip. I feel pressure in my chest. With it, a great wave of fear now fills my body. Drops of sweat build on my forehead.

I'm having a heart attack.

I manage to hold up my right index finger to the class and say, "I'll be right back" before I walk as fast as I can out of the room. I turn down the hallway and keep walking.

Where am I going? Who can help me?

Walking seems to help, so I walk quickly to the faculty restroom and sit on the toilet seat. It doesn't take long before my stools come out like water. My stomach turns over and over. Finally, the diarrhea stops. My breathing is beginning to slow down, but my heart is still racing. The pressure in my chest has lessened some. As I sit, I pray for peace.

After a few more minutes, I feel a bit better. I leave the restroom and walk down the hall to get a drink of water from the fountain.

Can I make it back to my classroom and get through this class? Can I make it through the day? Should I see a doctor before I get home?

I decide I can at least make it through this class; thankfully, lunch is next, so I'll have a break and figure out what to do next.

October 1992

I continue to be gripped by fear.

Scott has convinced me that since the episode in my classroom was a one-time occurrence that went away after about twenty minutes, my heart and my body are fine. I want so much to be strong for him and for everyone else. I can't let my husband, my kids, and my students down.

And then there's my mother, who is now at the Southaven Nursing Center, whom I feel I must visit each week; there's nobody else but me and Scott in her life who will visit her. But our kids are four and seven, and since my mother has never been a fan of Scott, and his presence may send her over the edge again, I often tell him to stay home with David and Analise.

How I love teaching my classes at this creative, high-energy school, and it seems like my students enjoy me, too. Within a few months, one of my students asks if I can help her start a literary magazine, and a few other students ask if I can be the faculty sponsor of a highly creative group called Odyssey of the Mind. Since I particularly relished my post-graduate studies in creativity, I agree to lead them; I love my students and don't want to disappoint them.

But as my pressure to perform mounts, so does my fear.

One Friday afternoon, I leave school quickly so I can drive ten miles east to spend some time with my mother-in-law, our children's *abuela,* a vibrant Hispanic sixth-grade teacher who lives alone in East Dallas. As I get into my car, I suddenly feel a great wave of fear move through my chest. I tell myself that I'm fine and that the fear is in my head.

I start the drive down the I-30 freeway. With each mile, I feel worse. Now I feel pain not only in my chest but also in my left arm. My stomach is turning over, but this time, there is no bathroom close by. I have read about the symptoms of heart attacks in women; I know this is the real thing.

Rather than drive to my mother-in-law's home, I drive myself to the Emergency Room at Mesquite Community Hospital. With my dizziness, it's tough to get out of the car, but I finally manage. I slowly enter the lobby and walk up to the check-in desk. A nurse looks up and asks me how she can help.

"I think I'm having a heart attack."

Quickly, other nurses surround me, and I'm put into a wheelchair and whisked down the hall to have my vitals taken. My blood pressure is 190/110. They ask me if I have any family members to call, and I give them Scott's number. In a few minutes I learn from them that he is on his way from Greenhill School, which is on the opposite side of town. He will drop our kids off at his mom's house first and be with me as soon as he can.

During the next half hour, I'm given many medical tests that rule out my having a heart attack. Gradually my blood pressure returns to normal. My blood work comes back normal.

What is happening to me?

An hour after I check in, Scott shows up, and when he walks into the room, I immediately feel a great wave of relief. His inner strength and presence have always helped me relax. I tell him about what happened, and he listens intently. He, too, is relieved that they have not discovered anything wrong with me. A few minutes later, a young female doctor joins us.

"Christine, since there is nothing conclusive that proves that there is anything wrong with you, and since your blood pressure is now almost back to a normal level, the other doctor and I believe that you have had a panic attack."

"*A what?*" I have never heard this term before.

"Let me explain to you what they are. Panic attacks are pretty common; about five percent of the adults in the United States experience panic attacks at some point in their lives. An individual can either have a stand-alone attack or experience multiple attacks over time, known as a panic disorder. Panic attacks are more common in women than they are in men and can materialize when people are perfectly calm or when they are anxious about something going on in their lives. And as scary as they feel, panic attacks aren't life-threatening."

"I'm sure glad to hear that," I respond.

"What has happened is that your body's sympathetic nervous system has ignited a 'fight or flight' response, even though there may not have been anything to fight or flee from. You also need to know that because panic attacks are unpredictable, you may be afraid about having future panic attacks. You'll need to get help for this fear as many people find the fear to be debilitating and to have a significant negative effect on their lives."

"What causes a person to have a panic attack in the first place?"

"Stress can be one cause of panic attacks, but genetics and a person's temperament may also play a role. Panic attacks can also be triggered by having a family history of anxiety or mental illness."

When I hear those last words come out of her mouth, I freeze.

A family history of anxiety or mental illness.

Throughout my life, my greatest fear has always been that someday I would end up like my mother. Once I moved out of her house at fourteen, I tried my hardest in every way to be as different from her as I could possibly be. And now this.

"From your symptoms, Christine, it looks like you have a 'textbook' case of anxiety. You need to find a counselor who can help you learn some techniques to deal with it. You may also find some relief from therapies like meditation, deep breathing, and muscle relaxation. I'm also giving you a prescription for a drug called Ativan. If you have more anxious feelings, just take one pill, and it should quickly calm you down. But I still want you to find a counselor who specializes in helping people with anxiety disorders, OK?"

I nod.

Scott and I leave the hospital a few minutes later. As we drive to his mom's house to pick up David and Analise, we silently hold hands.

November 1992

A few days later, I find a female counselor on my insurance plan and make an appointment to see her on the following Thursday afternoon. As the session gets closer, the thought of getting help from a counselor feels more and more awkward. For years, I have been the "together" one for so many people and have given counsel to my students, friends, and family members; do I really need this type of help? Can't I figure this out on my own?

On Thursday afternoon, I'm welcomed into a stark-looking office in North Dallas. A middle-aged woman introduces herself and asks me to sit down on a loveseat that is close to her winged-back chair. After reading over my chart, she asks me to describe the situation leading to my recent panic attack. She listens intently as I describe the fear that I've been experiencing for several months.

"Often fear is triggered by other stress-producing situations in your life," she says. "How is your relationship with your husband right now? Are you happy at work? Have you recently had any discord with anyone close to you?"

"My life is really pretty perfect. I have an amazing husband, two wonderful young children, and a great job. The only negative thing is that I probably have too much on my plate each day, especially since I feel responsible for my mentally-ill mother's wellbeing. When I was in the hospital a few days ago, they gave me a prescription for Ativan, but I'm afraid to take it. My parents never allowed me to take any medication during my childhood, so whenever I take any now, I always have side effects from it."

"Why don't you just carry the Ativan with you in your purse to use as a safety net? For many of my patients, just knowing that the medication is there keeps them from having anxiety about having another panic attack. And before we meet again, I want you to do something else, Christine. I want you to spend some time thinking about your past and if there was something that occurred in it that may be triggering your fear."

I tell her I will.

My past. For the past twenty years, I've been trying my hardest not to think about it. But if I'm going to understand my anxiety, I know I must return to that dark place. There is only one person alive who experienced some of the same childhood I did—my brother Paul. I'm not sure if Paul can help me, though, because he always felt much closer to and more loved by Mother than by Daddy. But even when acknowledging the disparity between our feelings towards our parents, I know I still must call Paul and tell him what's been going on.

I settle into the comfy green reading chair in our living room, take a deep breath, and dial Paul's number. He picks up on the second ring. "Hi, Sis!" he exclaims.

We make our usual small talk about how our families are and how our jobs are going. After a few minutes, I tell him in a more serious voice that I need his help.

"Oh…wow. I'll try my best."

I tell Paul about my fear these past few months and about my recent panic attacks, trips to the ER and counselor, and the charge that the counselor gave me: What is the root cause of my fear, when seemingly, with the exception of my still being responsible for my mother's welfare, everything else is going well in my life?

"When did you start to feel this fear, Christine?"

"It started this past summer after we had moved into our new home in our great neighborhood. Then out of nowhere, I got called to apply for my dream job teaching at the Arts Magnet High School. We also learned that Analise was accepted into the preschool at Greenhill School. It's so perfect right now, Paul, because all three of them get to go to this great school together every day."

He then asks one of the simplest, yet most important questions that I have ever been asked: "What were you afraid of?"

Without even missing a beat, I reply, "That it was all too good. That people might be jealous of me and wish something bad on me."

As soon as these words come out of my mouth, I know exactly where they originated—from our mother!

Throughout our childhood, whenever anything good occurred in our lives, whether our family bought a new car or I would tell Mother about a high grade I had earned on a test, she would say, *Kina Hora*, which in Yiddish means "Stop the Curse." And she had spent most of my life trying to stop the curse with her obscene hand gestures and gross body movements.

Without knowing it, I had internalized her fears, and now at the age of thirty-five, I was feeling the effects of my fear.

As I tell Paul about this huge revelation, I am overwhelmed by how logical my fear has been. Then Paul reminds me that our daddy's family history didn't help the situation, either, as Daddy had told us that he was raised in a superstitious Italian family that believed in "the evil eye." His mother used to look down and spit whenever she thought that a jealous person was wishing evil on her or on someone in her family.

When we hang up a few minutes later, I sit in the chair unable to move. Then, I slowly lower my head to my knees and say a prayer of thanksgiving. The root cause of my fear and anxiety has been found. And this knowledge will hopefully give me the power to understand it and better deal with it for the remainder of my life.

After a few minutes, I rise from the chair and walk out of the living room. I must tell Scott.

July 1993
Age 36

Laundry

I usually hate folding the white clothes
Your endless t-shirts
needing to be turned inside out
Your underwear
twisted and tossed
So few pieces of the white laundry are ever mine

But today you are gone
and I am delighting in folding your t-shirts
as I imagine your strong chest
filling each one up
your soft curly hair peeking out
I touch your underwear
and imagine us joined completely again
Your body so willing
Your heart so tender
Your love so pure

These parts of you
without the you
I long to touch
even now
so soon
so right

March 1994

Hope. I've always loved both the sound and meaning of that word. And now that President Bill Clinton is leading our country, I feel more hope than ever that we can turn some of this socio-economic disparity and bigotry around. And like so many, I love that he was born in a city in Arkansas called Hope.

In honor of his presidency, we decide to take a spring break family road trip to Arkansas and visit his birthplace. While in Arkansas, we plan to visit Hot Springs National Park and stay two nights in a condo on Lake Balboa in Hot Springs Village, where we'll rent a pontoon boat and do some swimming and fishing.

It's great to be on the road again with our kids. Despite being only five and eight, they already seem to be hooked on the adventure called traveling. On the first day, after getting off the main highway, we drive through a few winding country roads before we arrive in Hope and find Bill Clinton's first home. Both the city and his home are very humble. There's a simple sign marking "President Bill Clinton's Birthplace" in front of what looks like a wood-framed, three-bedroom house. We learn that he lived there with his grandparents for only the first four years of his life, but it's still special to see it.

Since we ate a late breakfast, we think that our usual "snacks and treats" will keep the kids full, but in the middle of the afternoon on the way up to Lake Balboa, the kids tell us they're hungry. Maybe we should find a place to eat an early dinner.

We still are enjoying our drive through the beautiful smaller towns in Arkansas, so we hope we'll eventually find a place to eat. We do. Ana's Country Kitchen.

It's almost 3:00 p.m. when our family walks into this small country restaurant. As we enter, we notice that the people who are seated turn to watch us as we walk to a table. We see a couple of waitresses look our way, so we assume that we'll be handed menus soon. The restaurant is quiet, but we can hear muffled sounds coming from the back kitchen. After a few minutes of sitting there and not being given a menu, I look for the person in charge. I now see an older woman at the front counter, so I rise and ask her for some menus.

"Here you go," she tells me, as she rudely tosses a few menus onto our table without even looking at us. We begin to decide what we want to order.

"I want a cheeseburger," David announces.

"Me, too," Analise says.

"Okay. When the waitress comes, we'll order them."

We wait. And wait. No one brings water. There are no place mats or silverware wraps.

Both David and Analise begin to look around.

"Where's the waitress?" Analise asks.

"Look, Mom! That family over there came in after us, and they are already getting their food! I'm hungry. When are we gonna order?" David looks around expectantly.

Even though they are in my line-of-sight, not one waitress looks our way or approaches us. The woman who had given us the menus is standing by the front counter. When I turn to get her attention, I see a look of disgust on her face, and she quickly looks away.

"Christine and kids—I think that these backward, ignorant people are discriminating against us," Scott says. "Maybe we just need to go."

Oh, my God! I never thought this could happen!

Scott gets up. "Let's get out of here," he says in a loud voice. "It's clear that we aren't wanted here and that these people don't deserve our business."

October 1995

How I love going to school each day! I'm finding it so exciting and fulfilling to teach, advise, and travel on trips abroad with my diverse and creatively driven Arts Magnet High School students.

Using my training in gifted education, I create a teaching mantra that graces the front of my colorful classroom that helps me be a better catalyst to bring out the creativity in my students: *I tell you what; you tell me how.* It is so gratifying to watch my students develop the most amazing "how's" to just about every assignment I give.

At the end of the 1994-1995 school year, I'm recognized for my teaching creativity and am voted the school's Teacher of the Year. Then I learn I've been nominated for a couple of other teaching honors—one being the most prestigious national teaching award: the Walt Disney American Teacher Award. Since the award includes an all-expenses-paid trip to Walt Disney World, a place that I really want my young children to see but know we can't afford, I decide to take the time and complete the necessary application forms.

After getting through several rounds in the application process, I learn that miraculously, I've been selected as one of thirty-six teachers in the nation who will be honored, both at Walt Disney World and in Washington D.C.—but unfortunately, Walt Disney and McDonald's who are sponsoring the event will pay for only one adult, not for my children, to accompany me on the almost week-long event.

There is no doubt I'll invite Scott to join me; the fact that he is also an educator makes my choice that much easier. Recently, I became even prouder of him because after being the Head of the Upper School at the Winston School for two years, he moved back to full time teaching—this time at the highly acclaimed St. Mark's School of Texas. He had missed being in the classroom with students and had lost the urge to pursue administration further.

In late October, Scott and I leave our two young children with his mother, their doting *abuela*, for the duration of the six-day event. We have never left them for this long, but there simply is no other choice to make.

We are flown to Orlando where we stay at the posh Grand Floridian Hotel for several nights. The first night we're there, I, along with thirty-five other finalists, am asked to make a three-minute presentation on why we teach. After these presentations, the field will be narrowed to twelve finalists, each in a different discipline, who will be honored at the end of the week in an Academy Awards-like ceremony in Washington, D.C.

The stakes are so high now as the twelve finalists will receive even more money, not only for themselves, but also for their schools. And they even will be awarded with a beautiful bronze sculpture with their name etched into it.

For several weeks, I've been preparing for this presentation. After musing about it for a while, I decide to tape my six-year-old daughter's elementary piano-playing of "Twinkle, Twinkle Little Star," juxtaposed with my nine-year old son's rendition of "Ballad," along with my brilliant student Victor's original composition for the piano.

They each play in the background as I speak about how the best teachers bring out this natural progression toward growth and creativity in their students. I end my three-minutes by saying, "There is no greater joy than to be the catalyst for more Victors in the world. We as teachers are the composers, and we have an enormous body of beautiful music, our students, to work with. We have the awesome responsibility of creating lifelong learners who will leave our classrooms and say at the end of their life journeys, like the Spanish artist Goya said at age seventy-six, *Aun Aprendo*—I am still learning. I also believe that there are thousands of people in other professions who are looking to find fulfillment in their work...teaching is what you should try doing; follow me. They may eventually come to believe what I have suspected for a long time: Teaching is one of the most noble professions a person can pursue."

The presentation goes well, and afterwards, I realize the risk I had taken in bringing a soundtrack as the background for my words was probably a good idea as no other presenter did anything like this. For the remainder of the week, all the finalists and their guests are treated to the absolute best of Walt Disney World and Epcot Center, including the newly opened Disney Institute.

Wherever we go, we're followed by a large entourage of reporters and filmmakers who chronicle our every move and make sure that we are the first ones on the rides, or if we aren't, that the lines and attractions are cleared for us; who get the behind-the-scenes tours; who have a fireworks display in our honor; and who literally have a red carpet rolled out for us before several of the events.

One morning as we are herded to yet another event, I hear a spectator ask one of the cameramen, "Who are *they*?"

"Teachers," the cameraman responds.

"*Teachers? Oh, wow...teachers.*"

How extraordinary it is to be treated like we are some of the most important people in society. In my heart, I know this is the truth.

After we spend four days in Orlando, we're flown on a chartered plane to Washington D.C. where we stay at the historic Hay Adams Hotel, a five-star hotel located directly across from the White House. That night we are treated to dinner in the Library of Congress, complete with a live orchestra that provides our background music, and the next day, we're taken to the newly opened U.S. Holocaust Memorial Museum.

And then, the final night comes—the night when we are recognized in the Warner Theatre. Each of us can invite four more people to join us at the event, so I invite my brother Paul, his wife Elsie, and their two grade-school children, Tim and Sara. As they live in New Jersey, the trip to Washington, D.C. is not too long for them to make.

My nerves have begun to tighten. What if I'm the English/Humanities winner? How can I possibly make a speech in front of tens of thousands of people, people who are both at the event and who are watching the telecast from around the world? The two other finalists in my category are a deaf teacher who teaches English to hearing-impaired children and a Native American woman who teaches English to a diverse population of students in the Southwest.

To prepare for the evening, each of us is taken a day ahead of time to be fitted for a custom evening gown, complete with the jewelry that works best with it. I've made a reservation to get my hair and makeup done for what will undoubtedly be the biggest night of my life. And then there is the matter of the speech that I must make if my name is read; just thinking of it sets my heart racing.

The morning of November 1st, I wake and find myself unable to eat the scrumptious hotel breakfast that is waiting for me. I'm afraid I'll throw up anything I eat. Scott and I go through the motions of the day making sure that we have a few hours of rest before my hair and makeup is done, and I get dressed for the awards show.

Early that evening, we are ushered into seats close to the front of the large auditorium. The speaker before the awards presentation is Maya Angelou, a woman who has been one of my heroes for many years. In the most perfect of coincidences, I have just taught her captivating autobiography, *I Know Why the Caged Bird Sings*, to my AP English classes. Vice President Gore is there to present one award, famous actors present other awards, and the award for English will be presented by the Head of the Department of Education, Richard Riley.

As we take our seats, I feel so proud to have Scott with me as he knows firsthand how important it is to be a full-time teacher once again. I take some slow in-and-out yoga breaths and say a prayer that I have prayed throughout my life. If I am selected the winner, "May the words of my mouth and the meditations of my heart be acceptable in Thy sight."

One by one, we hear the names of the finalists, and then Secretary Riley walks up to present the award for the English category. I feel my heart skip a beat as I listen to his long introduction that includes an anecdote about his own high school English teacher.

And then he opens the envelope to reveal the winner...*Christine Nicolette Gonzalez.*

I feel like another entity has taken over my body as I rise from my chair and carefully make my way up to the stage. I begin my short acceptance speech: "Can you imagine what would happen if more corporations would invest in our children's future? I want to thank God for letting me know when I was five years old that I was called to be a teacher. What a tremendous gift it has been to be a part of this profession...It is my hope and my prayer that the thousands of you watching this show tonight will be motivated to join us in the most noble profession. Please know that it is never too late to make a difference in a child's life."

Richard Riley hands me the beautiful ten-pound bronze sculpture of a child sitting on a book and holding up the world. Miraculously, my anxiety and fear are gone, and I feel God's breath and light permeating my being.

The next day we fly back to Dallas, and I suddenly find myself a celebrity. The local papers and TV news channels have done special features about my award, and I am called by a local radio channel to be interviewed as its Citizen of the Week. I even have a few companies call to ask if I would endorse their products; this, I find unacceptable.

Throughout this entire week, my mother is in her own world at Southaven Nursing Center and doesn't know anything about what her daughter just experienced.

November 1995
Age 38

Love

It doesn't burn anymore.
Now it's deeper and
more carefully seasoned.
I feel it for things
I never thought I would,
like for my neighbors who take
time to decorate their houses
for Christmas and for
my students whose
words add so much to each class.
I know I give it too easily
and sometimes I run dry.
But then you offer to
tenderly rub my swollen feet
with sweet almond oil
and somehow
I am whole again.

February 1996

It is late Tuesday afternoon after a long day of work, and Scott and I are on the highway headed with our kids to visit one of our favorite restaurants in Oak Cliff, La Calle Doce. My cell phone rings. I don't recognize the number but decide to answer it.

"Hello?"

"I'm looking for Christine Gonzalez," I hear a voice say.

"This is she," I respond.

"Christine, your mother, Sophie Nicolette, has just expired."

"Excuse me?"

"Yes. She had fallen from her bed. We called the ambulance, and on the way to Methodist Hospital, her heart stopped beating. They tried to revive her but couldn't. I'm so sorry. You need to go to Methodist Hospital to identify her."

I hang up and tell Scott the news. In the backseat, David and Analise, now eleven and seven, have heard my words and quickly stop talking to each other.

"What should we do?" I ask.

"I guess we should go to Methodist Hospital and identify her. I know how hard this is for you. I'll do it. You can stay in the car with the kids, okay?"

Once again, Scott is my rock.

And what next? So much to set into motion. While Scott is at the hospital morgue, I call Paul and tell him the news. I also tell him I will need his help with the funeral service details since I will be in Austin receiving the Texas Excellence Award for Outstanding Teaching. The award will be presented to me on Friday night, and I'll give an acceptance speech after receiving it; for the last few days, I've been working on the speech. Even in her death, my mother has the worst timing and continues to throw my life out of alignment.

We never make it to La Calle Doce that night. Instead, we return home and begin the process of planning my mother's funeral. Thankfully, it's already paid for at Restland Funeral Home. Since I have already lived through Daddy's tough memorial service, this one doesn't seem that difficult to plan; in fact, initially, I only feel great relief.

Paul calls later that night and tells me that since Mother did not have any church associates or friends, he'll be glad to lead the service. I tell him that I'll find someone to sing a solo and someone to play the organ. The plans are laid except for one thing: Who will eulogize her? Who can?

Since Paul is doing so much, I tell him that I'll somehow find something to say about Mother's life. Unlike at Daddy's death where I knew I didn't have the emotional strength to eulogize him, ironically, I suspect talking about Mother will be easier for me. The service is set for Saturday.

The awards ceremony is beautiful and meaningful as I am one of ten high school teachers recognized for excellence in Texas. Several members of my extended family, including Scott's mom and his brother Steve and wife Socorro, who are all teachers, have ventured down to Austin to support me; it means so much to have them here, especially during the emotional roller coaster of the past week.

We leave late Friday night and head back to Dallas, so we can pick up Paul at the airport on Saturday morning and then prepare for Mother's memorial service at Wildwood Chapel at Restland on Saturday afternoon.

There is one thing left to do: I must decide what I will say in this speech—my second one in two days. It's so tough to sort through my mixed emotions as I've lost the person whom I'd wished all my life I could love.

February 1996
Age 38

Your Gifts to Me

Was it only physical?
Like you
my bones and calves are large
my brown hair curly and thinning
my metabolism sluggish.
What were you that I can sing?

Nylon Shelton Stroller size 14-24 dresses
size 6EEE Revelation sandals
absent front teeth
a constant urine smell.

But you did obsessively tweeze your eyebrows
and with a toothpick
clean the brown wax from your ears.
Were these the only actions
that gave you pleasure?

Once as a child of ten
I opened the top drawer of
your brown dresser
hoping to stumble upon
some womanly secrets—
something that would make you
be a real mom.

All I found was an unopened
dark blue bottle of Evening in Paris perfume
nestled among two white handkerchiefs
and your pitiful unworn panties.

My Eulogy for my Mother
Age 38
Restland Memorial Park
February 17, 1996
(thirty-five people in attendance)

Sophie Rose Pines Nicolette: January 14, 1916-February 12, 1996

As some of you are aware, my mother Sophie was mentally ill for most of my life. I have often been asked how it was possible for me to become the woman I am today when I had a mother like this for the majority of my childhood. During the past few months, I have pondered this, too.

When child experts are asked what ingredient is the single most important one to give to a child, many mention love. When asked what time frame of a child's life is the key time period for growth and development, many mention the first five years of a child's life.

When I consider this, I know that Sophie Nicolette was an abundantly loving mother during most of the first five years of my life. She was forty-one years old when she gave birth to me. I remember hearing stories about how she nursed me for nine months and ground by hand every bit of food that I ate. She also wouldn't ever even think of leaving me or my brother with a babysitter as her greatest joy came from mothering us.

Yes, she had an obsessive love for me and Paul before she got sick when I was five, and that obsessive love transferred into our being loved and cared for more than most children. Clearly, these earliest years of my life positively affected me in more ways than I will ever know.

My mother also gave me a second gift that has been with me my entire life. At the earliest of ages, I remember hearing about God, and after a Vacation Bible School's puppet show, I walked forward at the end with a few other kids to say that I "was saved." My mother had an extraordinary hunger for anything that would increase her relationship with her Maker. From her influence, I grew up with a strong belief in God, and this belief continues to make a major difference in my life today. For this, too, I am indebted to my mother.

For the past three years, my mother has been blessed to live a relatively stable and happy life at a miraculous facility in far south Dallas called the Southaven Nursing Center, a psychiatric nursing center made particularly for people like my mom who it often seems have no place to live in our society.

Paul and I are especially thankful for the excellent care she received there—care made even more significant by a young man named Richard Lavallis who is a pallbearer today. Despite her deep prejudice towards black people—my mother was the only white person in this nursing facility—my mother loved Richard. She appreciated that he prodded her to try activities she normally wouldn't do, and it was Richard's care that she mentioned to me so often in the months before she passed. At Southaven my mom was also able to actively share her deep faith in God, something that always gave her the highest level of joy.

I want to close by sharing this thought with you. While I endured a lifetime of great difficulty due to my mother's mental illness, it is clear that the love and faith that she gave me during the first five years of my life were powerful forces that helped me to find the resilience to deal with what many would think was unthinkable trauma for a child to experience. For this I am grateful.

August 1999-May 2000

Since my mother passed away three years ago, I have immersed myself in the world of raising David and Analise. By 1999, due to the great burden of teaching 150 students, seventy-five of whom are in essay-heavy Senior AP English, and still having time to devote to my family, I feel my anxiety raise its head again.

For the past seven years, except for the summers, I've never gone anywhere without taking essays to grade—whether it was to a doctor's appointment or on any of the five international trips which Scott and I have taken with our students.

In 1999, I'm blessed to be hired to teach English at a reputable private school that is just a few miles from our home, The Episcopal School of Dallas.

That fall, my life quickly becomes more balanced as my teaching load is cut almost by two-thirds, and ESD's teacher-friendly schedule affords me much more time each day to plan and to grade. I also know that this is the right career move because the faculty and staff welcome me warmly and quickly make me feel like I'm part of their family.

But how I miss working with the creatively gifted and diverse students at Arts Magnet! Since I'm now only teaching freshmen, I also miss working with seniors and helping them discover their talents and what colleges might be their best fit.

It doesn't take long for Scott to once again be tagged as an administrator at St. Mark's; he now teaches only one English class and serves in a variety of administrative positions.

Analise, a fifth grader, has joined me at the Episcopal School of Dallas. She enjoys her new school and is quickly making friends. She loves to learn, and her teachers often tell us how much they love having her in their classes.

David, a Greenhill eighth grader, is an accomplished athlete, a musician who writes beautiful piano music, and an award-winning visual artist. Earlier this year, he entered a contest where he imagined and drew his vision of Downtown Dallas in the year 2050. He won first place and earned a $10,000 college scholarship. With his many talents, I often pray for wisdom to parent him wisely, so he'll have the time and resources to hone those talents.

July 1999

After eighteen days on the road, we're almost home from our 6,200 mile road trip to the Pacific Northwest. Princess Purr, our 1996 Chrysler Town and Country minivan, rocks! Never have we driven so many miles in such style and comfort, even going through ten states and British Columbia.

Since Scott had been a student at Oregon State University and fought forest fires on Mount Hood and throughout the Pacific Northwest, it was particularly meaningful for him to share this beautiful part of the United States with the three of us who had never been there before.

As we are about an hour out from Dallas, I decide to ask everyone for their top five list of memories from the trip. The youngest goes first:

Analise, Age 10

1. Throwing snowballs at David on Mount Hood on July 4th.
2. Seeing Multnomah Falls and the Rose and Japanese Gardens in Portland.
3. Getting truckers to honk their horns when I sat in the front seat of the van.
4. Meeting an old hippie doper who rented us a raft on the Rogue River and hearing Dad tell us afterwards, "Now kids, that's why you don't do drugs."
5. Watching Old Faithful erupt in Yellowstone National Park.

David, Age 13

1. Making up a language with Analise and then using it throughout the trip.
2. Being asleep for so many of the long drives—then arriving to a destination and saying, "That wasn't a long drive at all!"
3. Smelling the sickening sulfur smell of the Yellowstone geysers.

4. Forgetting to pack any underwear for the trip—and then losing a shoe when our van door opened.
5. The bizarre steam clock in Gastown, Vancouver.

Scott, Age 40

1. Watching the final of the Women's World Cup in a hotel room in Missoula, Montana. The US beat Japan!
2. Watching an eagle sweep down and pick up a fish from the Yellowstone River when we were on our way out. I told the kids that I had used my credit card to reserve the bird's performance.
3. Seeing Christine, "I love nature," in a tent. With an inflatable mattress, she complained that the ground was hard.
4. Meeting up with my first college roommate, Luis Vasquez, in Portland. I hadn't seen him in years, and it was great to meet his family.
5. At the Bonneville Dam, trying to explain the hydroelectric generators and salmon ladders to my family. They just didn't get why I was so excited about those scientific and natural marvels.

Christine, Age 42

1. Walking with Analise up the many stairs to the top of Multnomah Falls just in time to hear her say, "I got to pee!"
2. Seeing so much water: the constant flowing rivers outside our van, the crazy-blue water of Crater Lake, the breathtaking waterfalls, and the gorgeous Pacific Ocean.
3. Sharing a glass of wine with Scott at Timberline Lodge on top of Mount Hood while watching the kids play in the snow.
4. Portland. Everything about the city.
5. Sleeping with the family in a yurt for the first time and giggling with the kids while we listened to Scott snore.

May 2001

Scott hasn't found his vocation; his vocation keeps finding him. Due to his love for his school, his high respect for his excellent boss, and his ability to pinch-hit at so many positions, during the last few years, whenever there has been a need, Scott has agreed to take on whatever work Arnie Holtberg, the Headmaster of St. Mark's, has asked of him.

This year, he was the interim head of the upper school along with still being the director of studies, which included overseeing both the teachers' and students' schedules from fifth grade up. In addition, he taught a tenth-grade English class and served as an advisor to a group of students.

As the head of upper school, he also attended many of the high school extra-curricular activities, from athletic contests, to music and theatre events. As a result, he typically left our home between 6:30 and 7:00 a.m. and often did not return until 9:00 p.m. With David now a three-varsity-sport ninth-grader, and Analise, an active sixth-grader, I was often challenged to find time to be the best mother, wife, and English teacher I could be while keeping the kids fed and the house running smoothly.

On the first day of school, after getting my morning coffee I walked back to our bedroom to find Scott still lying in bed, curled up in a fetal position. When I asked him if he was okay, he turned his head over and whimpered, "I don't want to go to school." Already the stress was too much. Somehow, I convinced him to get out of bed and told him that he was probably suffering from depression; I would buy him some St. John's Wort later that afternoon.

In early December, I went out to the wooden cabinets in our garage to look for some holiday candle holders I thought were stored there. As I opened a cabinet and moved some glass jars, I came upon a bottle of opened Glenlivet Scotch Whiskey. It didn't have any dust on it. I then knew where the alcoholic smell that I sometimes smelled when I lay in bed at night must have originated. Later, when I confronted Scott about finding it, he confessed that he had begun to use alcohol to cope with his stress. He agreed to find a counselor who could assist him so he would be able to get through the remainder of the academic year.

Thankfully, the school year is almost over. It's a Saturday morning in late May, and Scott and I are excited that tonight we will be attending the Marksman Ball, the formal event that honors his school's graduating seniors each year. It's a tuxedo affair, so Scott recently purchased a black tux, and I bought an evening dress for the event that will be held at the historic Adolphus Hotel in downtown Dallas.

We begin the usual Saturday morning household chores. I leave Scott cleaning the bathroom while I'm out buying the weekly groceries. When I return an hour later, Scott helps me unload the groceries and put them away. Then he tells me that he needs to mop the kitchen floor. I leave the kitchen so he can work his cleaning magic; once again, I whisper a thank you under my breath to his mother who taught her kids, regardless of their genders, to do housework.

I'm in the bedroom when I hear Scott's voice cry out, "Christine!"

I rush to the kitchen and see him sprawled out on the tile floor.

"I just fell when I was mopping, and I can't get up."

"David! Analise! Come down to the kitchen now!" I yell up the stairs.

I hear them moving from their rooms and rushing down the stairs. We surround him in the kitchen, but our great big Daddy Bear is lying there motionless. He tells us his back has gone out, and he is in agony.

We aren't sure what to do. We know we can't safely get his 250-pound body into the car to take him to the Emergency Room, so I call his brother Steve who lives just a block away. Thankfully, he's home and says he'll be here in a few minutes.

I've never seen Scott's normally brown face turn white, but it now has. Steve arrives, and with his help, it takes all four of us to slowly pull Scott off the kitchen floor and move him into the front seat of our car. Throughout the process, Scott's deep moans tell us he is in agonizing pain.

I tell the kids that everything is going to be fine, but I need them to be brave and stay at home. I will call them as soon as I know anything. I begin to back the car down the driveway. Then I suddenly stop the car as it occurs to me that I probably should be driving Scott to a different hospital than to the hospital closest to us.

During the past few months, due to his stressful job, his chronic back pain had worsened. He had already seen Dr. Zigler at the Texas Back Institute in Plano several times. From our driveway, I leave an emergency phone message for his doctor and quickly get a call back telling me to drive Scott to Plano Medical Center, a modern hospital associated with the Texas Back Institute that is forty-five minutes north of our home.

From our experience, we both unequivocally know how important it is to always have the best doctor possible, so even though this is a longer trip, making the drive to Plano is the right decision. As we begin the journey, Scott's eyes have begun to roll back into his head.

Thankfully, the Saturday traffic is light, so the usual forty-five-minute trip to Plano is cut to thirty. I pull into the hospital entrance and follow the signs to the emergency room. I quickly get out and walk up to the desk and tell the receptionist that we need a wheelchair and assistance to get Scott out of the car. Two strong men follow me back to our car.

They quickly see what horrific pain Scott is in, so this expedites our admission. Before long, Scott is wheeled back to a small curtained area, and the tests begin. Dr. Zigler is called but can't be there for a while. Thankfully, he authorizes a morphine drip for the pain. I've never seen Scott in this much pain or his blood pressure this high; how much pain can he stand?

The hours pass by at a snail's pace, and nothing—even the morphine drip—seems to ameliorate Scott's pain. All the curtained partitions are closed; by the sounds around us, tragic events have struck in many other people's lives.

It's four hours before Dr. Zigler arrives. When he looks at the results of Scott's MRI, he tells us that if Scott wants to walk again, he must have back surgery. He needs to be admitted to the hospital and moved upstairs to a room as soon as one is available. When Dr. Zigler leaves, the ER nurse tells us there are no rooms available anywhere in the hospital. Scott needs to remain in the small, curtained area until a room is free.

I hate to leave Scott alone that night, but I must return home to care for David and Analise. Even though they are now fifteen and twelve, I simply can't leave them by themselves all night. Plus, I want to reassure them that once Scott has the surgery, all will be well.

When I visit Scott early on Sunday morning, he is seemingly asleep and still in the ER.

"Good morning, honey. How are you doing?"

He slowly opens his eyes and weakly replies, "Not very well. Even the morphine drip isn't helping much with the pain. I could barely sleep at all last night. And there were so many people all around moving, talking, and wailing. How are the kids?"

As I start to answer his question, a nurse comes in to check on him. I quickly ask her if any rooms have opened in the hospital.

"Not yet," she replies.

Scott and I sit together for several hours. I stroke his hand and forehead and pray that his pain will diminish. As I'm sitting there, I see a young man who had arrived in the emergency room earlier on Sunday being wheeled up to a room in the hospital. A trail of relatives follows him.

What?

I rise and look for our nurse. I ask her again about the availability of a room for Scott. She tells me once again that no rooms are available; she will let me know when one is. I tell myself that the young man's situation must be different from Scott's.

A little after lunch and after I have checked in with the kids at home, I see another person being wheeled upstairs to a hospital room. Something just isn't right.

By this time, Scott has been in the ER for over twenty-four hours. Everyone who has been moved to a room is Caucasian. Could it be that my Mexican-American husband is being discriminated against?

My cell phone rings. It's Scott's boss checking in again. When he asks me how Scott is, I pause as tears well up in my eyes.

"I don't know how else to say this, Arnie, but I think Scott is being discriminated against. He isn't being checked on very often, and they are still telling me that there are no available rooms for him.

But since we arrived early yesterday, I have seen two white patients who arrived hours after he did be taken to their rooms in the hospital."

I hear silence for a few seconds.

Then Arnie tells me, "Don't you worry about one thing, Christine. I will take care of this."

We hang up. I have no idea what Arnie intends to do to "take care of this," but just talking to him has given me hope.

Less than thirty minutes later, a nurse opens the curtains. She tells us that a room is available in the hospital now and that an attendant will be here shortly to wheel Scott up to it.

I am speechless. I feel a bitter taste in my mouth as anger begins to fill my chest.

My phone rings. It's Arnie. "Did you get that hospital room, Christine?"

"Yes—a nurse just came in and told us that Scott will be wheeled up to it shortly. I can't thank you enough for whatever you did, Arnie."

"I'm so glad it worked. There is nothing I wouldn't do for Scooter. And by the way, at the Marksman Ball last night, it was announced that the yearbook was dedicated to him. He is one loved human being."

September 2001
Age 44

Planeless Skies
(in memory of Lynn Tull)

A shadow
can be understood
but too many shadows
create a world
so dark
so void of hope
that one must wonder
why?

Yes
loonies exist who
crash their planes
into tall buildings
and kids make poor choices
to drive too fast
and lose control

But
how do you explain
a brain tumor inside
the head of an angel?

June 2002

The one thing we know about history is that it repeats itself. This certainly is true in my family. I remember an afternoon in the summer of 1971 when I needed a hat for a youth group costume party, so I went to Daddy's closet to look for one. Over to the far right was an object I had never seen before—a beautiful brush with a handle inscribed "made of Parisian ivory." In the middle of the handle was a large monogram with the initial *S*. I knew that Daddy's name, Charles, began with a *C*, so I had to ask him about it.

When Daddy came home, I showed him the brush.

"Why does this handle have an *S* on it, Daddy? Shouldn't it have a *C* for Charles or an *N* for Nicolette?

"Well, I guess you're now old enough to know this, Christine. That clothing brush was given to me by a woman named Pauline. She was my first wife. At the time, my name was Salvatore Joseph Nicoletti. I married Pauline when we both were very young. When I first met her, she was sick with a disease called syphilis, and I felt sorry for her. She was such a sweet woman, and she loved me so much, that eventually I grew to love her. She ended up dying in a mental institution a few years after we were married. As you know, it took me quite a few years to marry again, when I married your mother."

I couldn't believe what I was hearing. I didn't know whether to be sad about the death of his first wife or to be angry with him for keeping this important part of his life a secret from me.

"What made you decide to change your name?" I asked.

"When my parents immigrated to the United States at the end of the nineteenth century, the man who signed them in at Ellis Island changed the last letter of their last name to an *i*, so their Italian heritage would be recognizable. Because we were Italian, my large family faced discrimination. Many people thought we were 'dirty,' so we had to live in our own section of Brooklyn. As I got older, I knew that I would have a better chance of getting a job if I changed my name. When I married your mother, I made it official and changed my name to *Charles S. Nicolette*. Later, I learned that ending my name with an *e* rather than with an *i* was the way Nicolette was originally spelled in Italy. I'm so glad that I changed my name, Christine, as throughout my life it has helped people to not make incorrect assumptions about me."

When I was growing up, I knew my last name was a long one to write, but I loved the sound of it.

Nicolette.

Nobody had a last name like mine, and often people told me how beautiful it sounded.

When I married Scott in 1983, Scott wanted me to keep my last name. For our children's sake, I thought it was too complicated to do this, and at that time, it was also an unusual thing to do. So, I acquiesced to society's standards and dropped the name Nicolette without knowing the consequences that would result from becoming *Christine Gonzalez.*

With my last name now *Gonzalez,* one of the first things I realized was how many of my Hispanic colleagues befriended me more than they had in the past. Now they approached and often spoke to me in Spanish, trying to figure out if with my blue eyes, I was actually Hispanic. When I told them, *Mi esposo es Mexicano*, their friendly attitude towards me sometimes changed.

A few years ago, Scott and I needed a new car and ventured to CarMax to see an SUV we were interested in buying. The car was everything we were looking for at the right price. I quickly filled out the online loan application. A few minutes later, to my dismay, I was told we didn't qualify for the loan. How could this be? I had always prided myself in my conscientiousness with paying our bills on time and having a very high credit score. We certainly earned enough money to qualify for the loan and had lived in our home for many years.

When I inquired why our application was denied, the loan officer told me that when they entered my name into their system, many women with my name had poor credit. Before I could move further along in the application process, I had to prove to them that I wasn't any of the other Christine or Christina Gonzalezes who had poor credit. I turned to Scott in dismay. No way would we purchase a car from a company like this.

A few months later, we needed a new desktop computer and entered an Apple store to purchase one. Once again, despite both of our high credit ratings and good jobs, our application was denied due to my name being associated with the many Christine, Cristina, and Christina Gonzalezes who had problems with their credit.

Last year, I got to see first-hand the discrimination Scott experienced in the Plano hospital because his last name is Gonzalez. When I need medical care, I sure never want to be treated like less of a person because of my last name.

Currently, there are three other people employed at my workplace who have the surname of Gonzalez or Gonzales—two of them are even Christines! How nice it would be to not receive their phone messages or mail anymore.

Ultimately, I miss being a Nicolette because that was Daddy's name—the man whom I still greatly miss. It's time to see his name again every time I sign mine. But because of my marriage to Scott, I want to keep his surname name, too. I decide that Nicolette-Gonzalez will be my new last name.

I do some research and learn that for $500, I can complete the necessary paperwork to add an official hyphen to my name. The process is quite time consuming, but in a few months, the paperwork is complete, and my official name becomes *Christine Elise Nicolette-Gonzalez*—yes, a long name to write.

But what will my teacher-name be? Isn't Mrs. Nicolette-Gonzalez too big of a mouthful? I decide I'll be called Mrs. N-G for short.

That August on the first day of school, I introduce myself to my students as Mrs. N-G, and the name quickly sticks. In time, it even sounds endearing.

In future years, what a relief it is to see the name *Nicolette* on my door when I'm in the hospital facing several surgeries. But what about all the other Hispanic people who can't become a Nicolette and must deal with the discrimination their names often bring? I once again feel my white privilege—this time, it's the privilege of going back to a name I'm confident nobody will ever make negative assumptions about.

September 2003
Age 46

Your Music in Me
(for David)

I sink into the soft green chair
and listen as my inner corners are given life
It feels like the music is coming from me
but when I look down at my still hands
I realize it is coming from you

Your music echoes my deepest longings
what I can't find words to express
The notes fill the room quickly
They bang off the cold tile floor
The angels on the shelf smile
as Spirit is everywhere
The cycle is now complete
only you have raised the bar higher
than I ever could imagine

August 2004
Before David Leaves for The University of Texas
Age 47

To my beloved David:

The writer Kahlil Gibran wrote that the two best things that parents can give their children are roots and wings. For the past eighteen years, your dad and I have tried our best to give you strong roots. Today, as you start this next chapter of your life, you will finally have the opportunity to use your wings. Hopefully, your wings will enable you not only to fly, but also to soar. Just in case you were wondering, these are the ten roots that your dad and I tried to instill in your life:

A Root of Faith in God...perhaps that will mean finding a church with other Christians whom you can get to know; it will mean that God and prayer are always there for you.

A Root of the Importance of Family...we love you and will always be here for you, no matter what you do or don't do; we hope that you will often find your way back to us.

A Root of Taking Care of Yourself...without enough sleep, a healthy diet, and regular exercise you won't be able to be your best and use your gifts to their fullest.

A Root of Reaching Out to Those Around You...not just to the kids you already know. You never know when you'll meet a person who may become your life-long friend.

A Root of Doing your Best Work Academically...including not procrastinating when it comes to studying and writing papers :-).

A Root of Using your Gifts and Talents to Their Fullest...piano/guitar playing, photography, drawing, so many sports, sensitivity...wow...what a bouquet of gifts God has given you!

A Root of Integrity...telling the truth is always best; please never forget this.

A Root of Laughter...you have learned this root well; it always is a joy to be around you. I'll miss laughing with our family as you tell your fun stories.

A Root of Adventure...travel and spontaneity are two of our highest pleasures; we suspect you have come to crave them, too,

A Root of Service to Others...As Jesus said, when you do something for those who are less fortunate than you are, you are doing it for His glory.

It has been such an honor to watch you grow into the talented, kind, hilarious, and caring young man you are today. Words can never express the magnitude of how much I will miss you. I love you, believe in you, and will be praying for you every day.

With all my love,
Mom

April 2005

Our house stops vibrating the day David leaves home. After he graduates from ESD in 2004, David begins to slowly immerse himself in the world of advertising in the Texas Creative Program at the University of Texas at Austin. We all miss him a great deal, especially Analise, who is so close to him and who still has three years of high school left. But her active school life keeps her busy as she participates in student government, journalism, and choir. In her free time, she plays field hockey, lacrosse, and works out. Teachers continue to love her presence in their classes; she ends her freshman year by receiving the highest award of distinction.

As much as I hated leaving the creative world of the Arts Magnet High School, moving to ESD was clearly the best decision for our family; our kids have been so happy there and my anxiety issues have been minimized.

But another lingering issue from my childhood trauma continues to challenge me: food

Not only have I inherited my mother's slow metabolism, which made it very easy for me to keep extra pounds after each of my children was born, but I also share her tendency to overeat and to binge on sweets. Consequently, I'm now at the heaviest weight of my life, 211 pounds. Despite my many accomplishments, due to this high weight, my self-esteem has plummeted.

It's during an Ash Wednesday chapel at ESD that I make a decision: This time I will succeed at losing all my extra weight. I pray hard and often and know that if I can resist sugar for the forty days of Lent, I'll not only lose weight and feel better, but I'll also have the willpower to continue my weight-loss journey.

I manage to avoid sugar for the first week, but then temptation strikes. After a challenging day in the classroom, I'm beat. I walk into the teacher's lounge to check my mailbox and see a plate of homemade peanut butter thumbprint cookies with chocolate kisses on top of each one—my dream cookie. As in a trance, I walk up to the table and grab two cookies off the plate. Nobody else is in the lounge, so I quickly shove them into my mouth. Oh, God...how I have missed this taste! I walk to my mailbox and remove the memos inside. Then on the way out of the lounge, I quickly grab three more cookies. I consume them before I reach my car.

I am a Lenten failure.

During the remaining days that lead up to Easter, I find myself giving in to sweets several times. It's simply too tough to avoid sugar. And after each sugar binge, I hate myself even more.

A few weeks later, it's finally Easter Sunday. I know I must go to church, but I don't feel worthy of being there. As I'm getting dressed for the service, tears are already welling up in my eyes. I decide that I must focus on others, not on myself.

A few minutes later we arrive at Royal Lane Baptist Church, an inspiring, progressive church that has been our church home since David was in the seventh grade. As I get out of the car with Scott and Analise and begin to walk across the parking lot and then into the church lobby, I feel a few tears on my cheeks. I excuse myself quickly and head to the restroom in the back of the sanctuary. Thankfully, it is unoccupied.

I sit down on the toilet seat, and before long, my quiet tears have turned into vocal sobs. How can I do this to myself and to God? Why am I so weak that I cannot, even with so much prayer, have the self-discipline to give up sugar for just forty days of my life? I must get some professional help. On what should be the most triumphant day of the year for me as a Christian, I absolutely hate myself.

The next day I call my friend Janis and tell her about my difficult Easter Sunday. As always, she listens with the purest love and without judgment. Then she reminds me about Marty, a counselor she's been seeing regularly to help with some significant family issues. She tells me how much Marty has helped her and encourages me to give him a call—he may be able to help me, too. I have nothing to lose, so I get his number and leave a message for him on his voicemail. The next day, he returns my call, and we schedule a time for a late afternoon appointment; thankfully, it's in two days.

I walk into Marty's cozy office and introduce myself. He appears to be slightly older than I am and gives me a warm smile. He offers me a seat on a comfy couch. Then he takes a seat in the chair across from me and immediately removes his shoes. I think I'm going to like this guy.

I tell him why I am there—that I am really struggling with my self-esteem mostly because of my heavy weight. And we begin our journey together.

During the next few months, I learn a great deal from Marty. As I recount some of the trauma of my childhood and early adulthood, he helps me understand that when I was thinner in my teens and twenties, it was due to my Mother's sexual hang-ups that I often heard her call me a whore; with her hyper-conservative Christian views, she was afraid of what my having an attractive body could mean.

In my early twenties, I acted on her fears through my sexual activity, and later in my life, I acted on them by overeating; these were the two areas of my life I knew my Mother could never control. Like many, throughout my life, I also used food as a type of self-medication in times of stress.

Ultimately, I learn that it is my choices that determine what type of life I will have, not my abilities. I need to make choices that love, honor, and respect me. Choosing to binge on sweets is definitely not a choice that does this.

I also learn that I have a part of my brain that can act like a CEO, my prefrontal cortex, and that is the part whose voice I must listen to.

I must not listen to the squeals of my reptilian brain, my brain stem, that wants quick gratification and doesn't know when to stop eating. When I choose to eat better and to move more, I am honoring myself.

I see Marty over a period of four months. In our last session together, he asks two questions I'll never forget: "Who do you know who is appreciably happier than you are? Is thinner really happier?"

For the first time, I am speechless.

August 2005
Age 48

Three Grown Hearts
(for Scott, Analise, and David)

I lie on your chest
in the silence
feeling your every breath
in the rising and falling beneath me

On the leather couch
in the room next to us
she lies her head
on his slight chest
and pretends to watch the movie
But her mind drifts off
to the sweetness of foreign lands

Two hundred miles away
he's finally at her place
so ready to see her
His pace quickens
The light in her window beacons
and later the light
in her green eyes

They lie down on the bed
The silence surrounds them
as he feels her every breath
rising and falling beneath him

August 2007
Before Analise leaves for Kenyon College
Age 50

My Dearest Analise,

I was recently thinking about how your early nickname "the-pass-around-pack" applies so much to your present life as well as to your early years. You have heard stories about how perfect of a baby you were... how we could give you to anyone who wanted to hold you and you would still be content. Last year, you sure proved this once again when you traveled 7,000 miles by yourself and studied for a semester in Australia.

One of my biggest blessings has been having the opportunity to see you live and suck the marrow out of each day of your life. I was delighted to watch your early attempts at ballet, gymnastics, piano, soccer, Odyssey of the Mind, ice skating, and hip hop. I was gratified when you made your profession of faith and Pastor Ray Vickrey baptized you. I was so proud to have you (and of course, your brother, too :-)) as an exemplary student in my ninth grade Honors English class. I have empathized with your passion to travel as we have visited numerous states and countries, including our recent cruise to the Great Barrier Reef and Lizard Island. I have marveled as I have watched you delight in hitting the field hockey ball. My heart has sung along with you as I have heard you sing in choirs at Greenhill, Royal Lane Baptist Church, ESD, and Barker College. I have felt more pride than you will ever know as I have watched you grow from a timid, girly-girl in lower school into the mature, independent moral leader you are today; what joy you have added to my life!

I can't begin to tell you how much respect I have for you. Already you have characteristics that I could only dream you might attain. Your high moral standards, authenticity, loyalty to your friends, great love of adventure and life, courage to try new things, deep faith in God, and unbelievable self-discipline are traits that make you truly exceptional. And you know the fun part is still ahead of you--the years when you will get to use these gifts to make the world a better place.

Analise, as you continue your life journey at Kenyon College, I trust we will always find special ways to connect and to call our own. My life wasn't complete until the day you were born. Watching you grow to be the young woman you are today has been one of God's greatest gifts to me. Namaste, Analise. The Divine in me honors the Divine in you.

With all my love,
Mom

May 2009

Scott has just turned fifty, and our family is off to spend a long weekend in Maine after celebrating our niece, Sara's, beautiful wedding in Philadelphia. I had heard that childhood ends the day a teen sets foot on his or her college campus; David and Analise's childhoods have certainly been over for several years now. With David now employed as a creative director in advertising and Analise now a sophomore at Kenyon College where she has created her own major called Comparative Global Identities, we know that our family's vacation time is running out.

Early in our marriage, Scott and I decided that by the time we turned fifty, we wanted to have visited all fifty states. For some people, this would be a lofty goal, but since Scott's family traveled on road trips every summer when he was growing up, and mine traveled by car across the country, we didn't have too many more states to cross off our lists. Maine is Scott's fiftieth state, just in time for his fiftieth birthday.

Even though we've been middle-class educators, we've always found a way to make traveling a priority. Clearly, traveling has been our "drug of choice." But traveling requires both time and money. As educators, we've been blessed to have the time. In my thirties, I learned that we didn't need a plethora of money if we could recruit enough students to take along with us on trips, so by now, even our children have been blessed to see most of the United States and many fabulous countries throughout the world.

It is so poignant for the four of us to spend this long weekend together. We enjoy our first lobster rolls and love getting our feet wet at beautiful Kennebunk Beach. We stay at the Seaside Inn, and the beach it's near happens to also be a dog-friendly beach. As four dog-lovers, we delight in seeing many lucky dogs romp in and out of the water each day. The rugged natural beauty of Maine is simply breathtaking, and the salty Atlantic Ocean reminds me of the happy days of my childhood spent at the beach.

Our family has always loved to laugh together, and this weekend proves that we haven't lost our touch. How proud I am of the young adults our children are becoming! Though there are many big life decisions ahead, at the end of the weekend, Scott and I return to Dallas confident we have done the best we can do as parents. The rest is in God's hands.

October 2010
Age 53

My Secret

My dog knows things about me
that nobody else does
and this worries me.
He sees me
when I'm alone
and tries to comfort me.
He rests by my side
and looks at me
with his human eyes.

My dog sees me do things that
nobody else sees me do
and he doesn't get angry.
Rather, he walks slowly over
and sits very still until
I feel like I can
look up again.

May 2012

It's final exam week at ESD, and thankfully the administration has scheduled the English exam to be given first; this will leave me a week to get the blue composition books graded before the final grades and comments are due. Since my sister-in-law Sylvia is having gall bladder surgery today, I'm glad my exam schedule will provide time for me to drive to the hospital and check on her.

That afternoon, I'm sitting at my classroom desk grading essays when I hear my cell phone buzz. I look at the number. It's my mother-in-law. I answer and hear a very weak voice.

"Christine? I fell on the kitchen floor, and I'm bleeding. My legs hurt, and I can't get up. I tried calling Scott, Steve, and Dennis, but they didn't pick up. I just called 911, and they're on the way. I told them to take me to St. Paul's Hospital because my doctor is there. Can you meet me there?"

"I'll be there in about thirty minutes!"

I hang up and say a prayer for her well-being.

As quickly as I can get there, I arrive at St. Paul's and ask the attendant where Anita Gonzalez is. I learn that she has already been wheeled to a partitioned room and medical tests have been ordered. When I find her room, she's lying in bed and is hooked up to an IV and several monitors.

"Hi, *Mija*. Thanks for coming. Do you know how Sylvia is doing?"

"I haven't heard anything yet, but I'm planning on visiting her as soon as I leave you, and I just heard from Dennis. He'll be here soon. You just need to rest right now. Once we learn what's going on with you, you'll get the medical care you need."

"Thanks, *Mija*."

I sit with her for the next hour as her test results begin to return.

Dennis arrives first, and it's great to see him. He loves to joke around and quickly has his mother laughing. I hang out for a while longer and then decide to visit Sylvia and see how she's doing. She's at Renaissance Hospital, about ten miles south of St. Paul's, so I head there.

When I arrive at the hospital, Sylvia is already sitting up in her bed. Thankfully, her surgery has gone well, and she isn't experiencing much pain. She is surprised to hear that her mom is in the ER at St. Paul's and is worried about her. Her fears are relieved a bit when I tell her that all three of her brothers are with her mom now.

A half an hour later, I head home and call Scott to let him know that Sylvia is doing well. He tells me that his mom's personal doctor is heading to the hospital. They should know more soon.

A few days pass—days filled with check-ins on both my mother-in-law's and Sylvia's health. Both have had some complications set in.

On Saturday, I know that Scott and I need a break from the heaviness of the week, so I suggest that we see a movie. We head to the Magnolia Theater to see *Silver Linings Playbook*. For a couple of hours, my mind is free from family concerns.

As we leave the theatre, the sunlight is almost blinding. I close my eyes, and suddenly I feel great pressure in my head unlike anything I've ever felt before. It seems to build with each step I take. By the time I arrive at our car, the pain has moved to my chest.

"Scott, something is very wrong with me."

"Do you think you're having a panic attack?"

"No. This feels very different. My head feels like it's going to explode. I think you better take me to an emergency room."

The closest emergency room is at Presbyterian Hospital, just a few miles away. But if I'm admitted to the hospital, that would mean that Scott would visit me in one hospital and visit his mom in another.

"Take me to St. Paul's," I tell him.

It takes just fifteen minutes to get there, but it feels like hours as my head pain increases with each mile. When we pull into the ER area, Scott quickly gets out and walks me in. He tells the attendant at the desk that I may be having a heart attack. Immediately, I'm wheeled to a room to begin some tests.

The first thing the nurses do is to take my blood pressure: 211/120—the blood pressure of someone who is having a stroke. I feel an IV needle pierce into my left arm, and my head begins to spin. Then I'm wheeled out for a chest x-ray. Due to my high blood pressure, they also want to do a CT scan. I see Scott for a few minutes; then I'm gone for yet another test.

After the tests are done, and I'm wheeled back to my room, the pressure in my head begins to ease a bit, but I am utterly exhausted. The nurse comes in and tells us that every test has come out negative and that a doctor will be arriving in a few minutes to talk to me. Scott is still sitting in the chair next to me when I doze off.

I wake to the doctor's hand on my right arm. "How are you feeling?"

"Very tired, but a little better."

"We gave you something to lower your blood pressure, and it has a sedative in it. That's why you're feeling so tired."

I turn to look at the monitor that automatically takes my blood pressure every fifteen minutes. The last reading was 150/90. Thank God, it's coming down. The doctor tells me to just keep resting and leaves the room.

A few more hours pass. I mostly sleep. Sometimes when I open my eyes, Scott is sitting next to me, and sometimes I'm alone.

Finally, I hear the doctor in my room and open my eyes. It seems like a day has passed since I was admitted to the hospital, but when I look at the clock, it's only 8:00 p.m.

"How are you feeling?"

"Better."

"Your husband told us that you have a history of panic attacks, right? Since all your tests have come out so well, and your blood pressure is now at a normal level, I suspect that your elevated blood pressure was a result of your anxiety disorder. Your husband also told us that you've been very involved in the care for his mother this week, and you've been worried about both her and your sister-in-law's health. You also have the pressure of getting all your work done to complete the school year, right?"

I nod.

"I'm going to send you home with a prescription for an anti-anxiety pill. I also suggest that you get counseling to learn some techniques that can help you with your anxiety so that this won't happen again."

It's been twenty years since I heard anything about my anxiety issues. I thought I had worked through all of them after learning how they were linked to my mother's *kina horas*.

What else can I do to get help now?

That night I log on to the computer and search "ways to deal with anxiety." I scan through the list of articles that pops up and see one on the benefits of knitting. Knitting? Wow. It would be great to learn to do something that could help me with anxiety and at the same time to create something—maybe even a baby blanket. David has been seriously dating an accomplished girl named Sally who works with him at Moroch Advertising; maybe they'll get married and have a child. Knowing how to knit a baby blanket would sure come in handy!

I search for knitting stores in the area and learn that Holley's Yarn Shoppe is close to my house. It even offers knitting classes on Saturdays. I'll call tomorrow and sign up for a class.

But that isn't enough; I also need to get some counseling. I remember how Marty Glass had helped me seven years ago, so I call and leave a message telling him that I need to see him again.

That's it; I've figured out my one-two punch. I'll do whatever it takes to never experience an anxiety attack again.

I begin to learn to knit on Saturday. Even though my hands are dexterous on the piano, I quickly learn that I'm "knitting-challenged." But I keep at it. Thankfully, I have some very patient teachers at Holley's. The shop owner, Susan, begins to teach me, and later I meet an employee named Suzuko who takes over where Susan leaves off. When I visit the shop and ask for her help to correct my many knitting mistakes, Suzuko and I quickly become friends.

Weeks later, I'm so proud when I finally complete my first scarf. The next time we visit our cabin in the mountains of Mena, Arkansas, I take it with me as I suspect I'll have more use for it there than in Dallas. Now that I've knitted one scarf, I start to knit another. By Christmas, I hope to give scarves as gifts to so many people who matter to me.

July 2012

> *It's a miracle that we are having this conversation in my office and not in a psychiatric hospital.* —Marty Glass

Marty welcomes me into his office with a kind smile and handshake. I feel like I've just entered a room in my home. I wait for him to take his shoes off.

He asks me how I've been, and I tell him that I definitely could be doing better. But then I realize that my current weight is eighteen pounds less than it was seven years ago. I tell him this, and he congratulates me.

"But of course, I still have a long way to go," I quickly say.

"Who doesn't?"

I nod and begin telling him the story of my recent anxiety attack that was triggered when I was called upon to assist with my mother-in-law's care. He listens intently as I speak, nodding a few times.

When I finish, he says, "So it sounds like you jumped in the water when you couldn't swim."

I hadn't thought about that. I think I jumped in the water when I thought I could swim, but I learned that I couldn't.

"If you are going to jump in the water to save someone, you need to know that you're equipped to do it," he tells me.

We talk about what it means to be equipped. Often that means taking care of yourself and being kind to yourself before you are kind to others. I think back to the lesson he had taught me seven years ago about doing this. There is so much truth to his words.

Once again, I see Marty for a few months. This time, I learn how to equip myself for the situations in life that often trigger my anxiety. When I have the fear of turbulence when flying, I can listen to calming music, sniff lavender oil, and bring along soft pillows—one to hold, and one to rest on. When I worry about possibly facing a bear on a hike in the woods around our cabin, I can attach bear bells to my shoes and take along bear spray just in case I confront one. When I don't think I'm strong enough to face the memorial service for a student who has committed suicide, I can journal and meditate ahead of time and practice deep breathing during the service.

Of course, there are times when illness or tragic events come on so quickly, like when my mother-in-law was rushed to the emergency room. I must remember to take care of myself during these times of unexpected stress; I don't always have to be the first one to jump in.

During the next few months, I share even more of my childhood trauma with Marty, and he tells me that it's a miracle I was able to survive and thrive as well as I have. After feeling so weak, it is affirming to have him remind me that I am a woman of great strength.

December 2013

The 6:00 a.m. alarm wakes us, and we hear the good news: Due to the ice on the roads, both of our schools are closed today. Despite our long teaching careers, experiencing a Texas snow day still feels like we have scratched off a winning lottery ticket. Simply not having to rush to get out of the house in the morning is a great gift.

So what should we do? After school today, we were planning to visit Scott's mom who is now in ICU in yet another hospital, this time suffering from a broken hip. Since we drive a Subaru that has all-wheel drive, now we can get out on the icy roads and visit her even sooner. I glance over at the scarf that I've been working on. What a great day it is to find someone who needs one! I walk to our gift closet and open the bin where I keep all my knitted items. Five completed scarves lie inside, and since I have already given scarves to all of my family members and close friends, there is nobody left to give them to.

At that moment, I hear an inner voice tell me to bring those extra scarves along when we visit Scott's mom in the hospital; maybe there will be some people who can use them.

Scott backs our car out of the driveway, and we head up the street.

"Can you drive by a bus stop? I want to see if there is anyone who might use one of these scarves."

"Sure."

We drive up the street a few miles from our home. I see a young, Hispanic man in a tan windbreaker waiting at the bus stop. He is huddled over and looks like he is freezing.

I tell Scott to pull the car over.

What will I say to him? Will he understand what I say?

I reach down and grab a grey scarf that I finished making a week ago. The car stops, and I roll down my window and motion for the young man to come to our car. He does. I reach out the window with the scarf in my hand, and the words that come out of my mouth are, "I made this for you."

"For me? *Gracias! Gracias!*" He takes the scarf, unrolls it, and quickly wraps it around his cold neck. As we pull away, I see him smiling.

"Now, I know why I'm knitting," I tell Scott.

We have four scarves left. It has become our mission to give them to the right people. A few minutes later, we pull into St. Paul's Hospital, and I see a nurse scurrying across the parking lot. She also looks underprepared for the onslaught of frigid weather as she isn't even wearing a coat. I tell Scott to stop the car. Once again, I roll down the car window.

"I made this for you," I tell her, as I hand her an aqua scarf.

"Oh, my! Are you sure?"

"Yes. Please take it. We hope it will warm you up."

I haven't had this much fun in a long time. But now it's time to check on my mother-in-law. Unfortunately, a scarf won't help her health to improve.

After the hospital visit, Scott and I return to the car and continue our quest of finding cold people who can use the final three scarves.

On the way back to our home, I see a man standing by a bus stop. He is using crutches and only has one leg. As I get out of the car and walk through a few inches of snow to get to him, he sees me coming his way carrying a brown scarf.

"I made this for you," I tell him. "I hope it will warm you up a bit."

"That is so nice of you. Thank you."

When I get back to the car, it's evident that Scott is enjoying this as much as I am. "Let's go by Fiesta Supermarket," he says. "There may be some people walking home from the grocery store who need a scarf."

"How do you say, 'I made this for you' in Spanish?" I ask him.

"*Hice este para ti*," he says.

I repeat the phrase enough times so when I hand out the final three scarves, the recipients will be able to decipher what I say.

When we arrive at Fiesta, we quickly find three more people to give the scarves to: a woman walking to her car in the parking lot and a mother and her young daughter walking home from the market.

Arriving back home, I feel the happiest that I've been in a long time. Giving these scarves to people who need them is the absolute best thing to do on this cold day—and a great way to use my new-found knitting skill. I must share this experience with Janis.

Later, when I call Janis to tell her about my amazing day, she is equally excited. Without my knowing it, that evening she shares my scarf-giving adventure with her mother, Arlene.

A few days later, Arlene tells her friends who knit at the Jewish Community Center what I did with my five scarves, and they decide they also want to knit scarves for people who need them. Then I learn that Arlene has also spread the story to the folks at Holley's Yarn Shoppe, and several people there want to join in. What I initially thought was just my desire to knit and give out scarves as random acts of kindness is quickly becoming something much bigger than this.

Later that week when I walk into Holley's, Susan tells me she would like to donate yarn to help us with our mission, but for her to donate yarn from her shop, I'll need to start a non-profit organization.

Could it be that my anxiety disorder is morphing into one of the most exciting opportunities of my life?

March 2014

For the past few years, Paul and I have intentionally shared a brother-sister weekend each year. This year I invited him to join me at Casa Verde—the beautiful cabin in the Ouachita Mountains that Scott and I were blessed to buy in 2010. Situated on twelve acres half a mile from the Ouachita River, and bordering the Ouachita National Forest, it is indeed a haven of rest and renewal. How wonderful it has been to catch up with each other and to speak our own special Nicolette language! And Paul understands the healing and transformation that simply being in this Edenic setting can bring.

Each morning, we linger over coffee and meaningful conversations. We talk about our childhoods like only we can. And empathy. And boundaries. And past mistakes, along with the joy of growth. He also helps me as I continue to build my vision for my non-profit, which I have decided to name Spreading the Warmth. Few know the world of computers like Paul does, so it's wonderful to get his advice on domain names and ways to build a website, something that I'll have to teach myself to do this summer if this non-profit is to become a reality.

It's Sunday evening, our last night together, and we have just gone to our respective rooms for the night. Tomorrow we will get into the car and head back to Dallas where he will depart for his New Jersey home.

I slip under the covers of the wood-framed bed and read a few of Mary Oliver's poems. Few write about nature like she does, and there is no better setting than Casa Verde to read her poetry. Soon I'm drifting off to sleep.

At 3:05 a.m. I'm startled awake. My heart is racing. I feel a rush of pressure in my chest. I quickly get out of bed and get a sip of water from the bathroom sink. My breathing is rapid, and my heart is beating so quickly and hard that it feels like it will burst out of my chest.

Oh my God...I need help! But how can I wake Paul and ask him to drive me through the dark, rough roads and around sixteen switchbacks just to get down the mountain? Will I die before we reach the Mena Regional Health System that's forty-five minutes away?

Sweat soaks through my nightgown. My head is spinning. I have no choice; I must wake him.

I walk out of my room and slowly tiptoe to the guest room on the other side of the cabin. I stand at his door briefly listening...for what, I don't know. Then I tap lightly—and then a bit more loudly and urgently.

I wait. I tap again and call out, "Paul?"

"Christine, is that you? Are you okay?"

"No. I need you. I'm so sorry, but can you come out?"

Paul slowly opens the bedroom door and quickly sees that I'm not in a good state.

"Hey, Christine. What's wrong?"

"I'm so sorry to wake you, but I think I'm either having a heart attack or an anxiety attack."

He puts his arm around me, and we move into the main room where he motions for me to sit down on the couch.

"When I feel like this, I can't sit down. I feel like running. I'm so scared. Oh, Paul, I'm so sorry that I woke you up."

Paul has always been great at offering comfort in times of distress, and this time is no exception. "There's no place that I'd rather be right now than out of bed and helping you get through this. I'm so glad you woke me up. I'd be upset if you hadn't. What are you feeling right now?"

When he asks me this, I feel like I'm finally able to sit down on the couch.

"Remember those panic attacks I had in my mid-thirties? Well, sometimes, seemingly for no reason at all, I still feel anxiety coming on me again. It's such a scary feeling. My heart starts to race, and I have a difficult time breathing. I feel like something really bad is going to happen to me."

As I tell him this, I feel my breathing returning to a normal pace and my heartbeat slowing down. Just having him here to talk to helps so much.

"Thanks so much for being here with me right now, Paul."

He reaches for my hand, and we share a moment of silent yet understood love.

Then he prays, "God, please help Christine right now. Give her peace. Let her feel your presence and know that she doesn't have to worry about anything. Calm her mind and restore her spirits. Let her feel my love and your love for her."

Already, I'm beginning to feel better. Paul asks if I would like to share a cup of tea and honey with him. There is nothing better that I can imagine doing.

May 2014
Age 56

The only time
my name was ever
carved into stone
it was spelled incorrectly.
So much for being immortal.

A few years later
they came and
plowed down the sign
and in its place put
an ugly black marble square
without life
breath or feeling.

It's so very clear
that I'm not supposed
to be immortal.

June 2014

School is finally out, and I intend to use the summer to systematically work through Hutton and Phillips' *Non-Profit Kit for Dummies*. When I give the book a cursory look, I quickly realize that starting a non-profit is an extremely time-consuming endeavor. Many forms must be completed, and with each step along the way, careful records must be kept. But I still feel called to start Spreading the Warmth; simply too many "coincidences" have occurred. I could even ask David who has just started an advertising firm, The Shop, to create a logo for it. I've already thought of its tag line: *I made this for you.*

The first task to complete is submitting the formation application to the Texas Secretary of State Office in Austin. Before Scott and I head to our cabin where we will spend several weeks, I put the completed application in the mail. I know that I will also need to build a website—something that I've never done before. But I have time, and if I've learned anything in life, it's this: If I keep plugging to complete a goal, the goal will eventually be accomplished.

Each day, I punctuate my hours of work to start Spreading the Warmth with long hikes through the mountains that surround our cabin. One evening, I get in my kayak and paddle out on our pond as Argie, our goldendoodle, swims alongside me. Several early mornings and evenings I ride my ATV on the miles of dirt paths that surround the cabin. Feeling the cool air hit my face as I cross the rocky Ouachita River and navigate alongside the innumerable towering trees gives me unparalleled joy.

It's the greatest gift to have this time, in this place, to work on this project. By the time the two weeks are over, I've completed most of the necessary steps to start Spreading the Warmth. I've also started to build the organization's website.

We return to Dallas a few days after my June 24th birthday. When we pick up the mail, I notice an official-looking envelope from the Office of the Secretary of State in Austin. I open it to learn that

Spreading the Warmth has already been approved. And the official formation day? June 24th—both my and Daddy's birthday! I want to believe that this, too, is much more than a coincidence.

August 2014

I spend many happy years teaching at The Episcopal School of Dallas, but due to a devastating lawsuit, during the past few years almost every person who had been in a leadership position has either stepped down or has left the school. I find many of the demands of the new administrators unacceptable. I feel my prized career slipping from my fingers as seemingly no part of my job is under my control.

With each new initiative, I feel my anxiety rise.

Intuitively, I know that not only is the new administration asking for far too much from its teachers but also that many of the new initiatives will not work. I'm charged to change the beloved curriculum I had developed over the past fifteen years; the number of sections and number of students I teach is increasing; the type of classes I teach is changing; the way I teach vocabulary—one of my most successful endeavors—is mandated to change; the amount of unscheduled time I have each day to work with my students one-on-one on their writing is decreasing, and there are new computer systems I must learn in order to take attendance, to keep track of my grading, and to write my student reports.

I know that many of these changes will make it difficult for me to be the best teacher I can be.

Anger and anxiety about these changes consumes me and often keeps me up at night. Knots form in my stomach, and I feel chronic gastric pain. For the first time in my thirty-five-year career, I am dreading returning to school.

I reach out to my new department head, my head of upper school, and to the director of employee services. I even decide to be totally vulnerable and share with them that with my anxiety disorder, I'm not sure my health will hold up throughout the new school year.

They each feel like their hands are tied, so they can't change anything.

Just before the 2014-2015 school year begins, on the second day of teacher in-service training I walk into the teacher's lounge and discover that my mailbox has been moved to the top row, and even on my tiptoes, I am unable to reach it. Next, I walk to my classroom in a building on the other side of the campus. When I arrive, I find that due to the carpets being cleaned, it has been emptied; the furniture, the computer, and all my personal possessions are now sitting in a huge disheveled mess in the hallway. I am unable to do the necessary planning for the year that I intended to do.

My mind flashes back to 97 Rumford Road. I've just returned from another day in fourth grade. I tentatively open the front door of my house and see scattered magazines and dishes lying in the mess of our living room. There is a fresh, dark puddle of urine on the carpet. I find her in the dirty kitchen and watch as her index finger moves back and forth from her nose. I can't stand it. I must escape before it consumes me.

Later, I sit through several long meetings, each one focusing on the new initiatives that will begin in just a few days. At the end of the last school year, to save money, the school "bought out" several of the strongest veteran teachers—two of whom are my close friends and confidants. Due to the great amount of change at the school, many other faculty members also left. Now, there is seemingly no one whom I can turn to for support.

When I walk into the general faculty meeting at the end of the day, a third of the faculty is unrecognizable to me. Once again, I feel alone. Most of all, I feel like everything is out of my control.

I return home with more knots in my stomach. Since the beginning of the summer, I had been experiencing so much gastric discomfort that my primary doctor ordered a colonoscopy to be done after in-service on the following Tuesday. Hopefully, the report will help me understand what is going on in my intestines.

I'm not able to rest very long because Scott has asked me to join him at the annual St. Mark's New Faculty Dinner. Even though I still feel a great deal of anxiety and stomach discomfort, I know I should accompany him; in the past, this dinner has always been one of my favorite events.

As we drive to the beautiful Highland Park home where the dinner is being held, I tell him how difficult my day has been and how sick I feel. As always, he listens in disbelief as he hears about the numerous changes at my school.

At St. Mark's School of Texas, it has been his experience that whenever a new expectation is added to a teacher's load, the administration tries to make an equitable adjustment elsewhere; consequently, the turnover rate at the school is always manageable. Clearly, they believe what I often have heard my good friend Katharine say: "Happy teachers make happy schools."

When we arrive at the dinner, I try to leave my school worries behind me and enjoy meeting the few new faculty and staff members who have joined St. Mark's. But on the way home, I feel my anxiety begin to rise again.

"I just don't know how I'm going to make it through this school year," I tell him.

"Okay, Christine. I need to tell you something very important. I am sick and tired of hearing you complain about your school. For months, I have listened to you, and right now it seems like your mind can't stop spinning, and your spinning is beginning to affect my mental health as well. You need to either shit or get off the pot. Either you do it, or you don't.

"Our kids are grown now. You know we don't spend our money frivolously. If you want to quit your job right now, you can do it. I promise to support you as you look for another job. We can cut our budget and just live on my salary until you get another job. I'm giving you my blessing to do this. But if you decide to stay at ESD, you must stop complaining every day about how terrible your situation is. I can't take it anymore.

"I'm going to give you till tomorrow morning to make up your mind. If you wake up and say you will stay at ESD, remember what I said about not hearing you complain anymore. If you wake up and feel that you need to leave, you will have my support; I will help you move out of your classroom this weekend. But since the school year will be starting a week from Monday, you need to make your decision tonight; anything else will make it that much harder for your school to replace you."

That night as I get into bed, I say a simple prayer: *God please let me know by tomorrow morning what I should do.*

At 3:00 a.m., I am suddenly startled from my sleep. I sit up in bed and feel great pain in my gastro area.

Maybe when I have my colonoscopy on Tuesday, they will find a cancerous growth, and I will have an easy way to back out of this school year! How I hope this will happen!

Immediately after thinking this, I realize the absurdity of what I've just thought. This is how sick my school situation has made me. I have no other choice than to do something I have never done in my entire life. At the age of fifty-seven, I must quit my job.

I wake up Saturday morning feeling lighter than I have felt in months. I am confident that I have been guided by a Divine Light and have made the right decision.

When I share my decision with Scott, he gives me a big hug and says, "I can't imagine how hard this decision was for you to make, Christine. Or how tough the situation was for you. You managed to live through twenty years of teaching thousands of public-school kids in Dallas's inner city. I never thought you would leave the profession this way."

September 2014

Just a few days after I quit my job, after she's been on a six-year roller coaster of health decline, my beloved mother-in-law dies from congestive heart failure and renal failure. Enduring the losses of both my job and my surrogate mother is an enormous challenge. Thankfully, my colonoscopy comes back normal, so now I am jobless but ready to attack finding a new career at an age when many people are close to retirement.

How employable will I be?

I quickly apply for jobs at local community colleges and add my name to substitute teacher lists at several private schools in the area. Since school is about to begin, every private school already has filled its English openings, and I know that at my age and in my current vulnerable health, I don't have the strength to go back to teaching in the public school system.

When my daughter Analise flies home from Colorado to attend the funeral services for her *abuela,* we spend some time together musing about my job possibilities. As a former Baltimore Teach for America high school teacher, Analise now supervises teachers and works for Teach for America in Colorado Springs. I'm so proud that she has also chosen to pursue a career in the field of education; her input right now is invaluable.

One afternoon when we take a walk around our neighborhood, we are stopped by Lisa, a good friend who has also been our family's tax accountant for many years. She asks me how school is going, and I tell her I've just quit my job and am looking for a new place of employment. She's extremely surprised to hear this as she knows how I had loved working at ESD, and as I had tutored her daughter Grace on several occasions, she also knows how passionate I am about working with students.

"Why don't you start your own tutoring business?" she asks.

I pause. I had never thought about doing this.

"I'd recommend you to so many of my friends. Parents of kids at Parish Episcopal School often look for tutors for their kids, and you're so good at it."

"Wow. I'll think about doing that, Lisa. Thanks so much."

By the time Analise and I arrive back home, with Analise's encouragement, I've decided to do it. Lisa's words are the divine intervention that I've been seeking.

I sure have always loved starting things. Since I was in my thirties, I've started an AP English program, a talented and gifted program, a literary magazine, and a variety of clubs at the schools where I worked; Sunday School classes at three different churches; and recently, the non-profit Spreading the Warmth, which would be hosting its first Knit Night later this month. David helped me with the branding of Spreading the Warmth; would he also help me design business cards for my tutoring business?

How great it would be to work for myself! I would be my own boss and would get to choose when I worked, where I worked, and with whom I worked. Having this much control over my career might also lessen my anxiety.

I launch into this new endeavor full steam ahead. What should I call my tutoring business? I remember that two of the most fulfilling years of my career occurred in my early thirties when I directed the Laureate Program for the Talented and Gifted at North Dallas High School. I have always loved the word *laureate* because of its Nobel Prize connotations. Laureate Tutoring. It has a nice ring to it.

With the help of Lisa and Facebook, I schedule my first student at Parish Episcopal School on September 9th. Then the calls begin to come. It helps a great deal that I've already established my reputation as an educator in the Dallas area.

By the end of September, I have earned $1,488. Parents tell other parents about me. I am asked to tutor another Parish student, this time every other day. A few days later, I begin to work weekly with my first St. Mark's student. In October, I earn $4,695. This is all the affirmation I need to know that a new chapter of my career has successfully begun.

December 2016
Treasure Island, Florida

Of the many surrogate mothers who came into my life once I left home, my final surrogate mother, my "Mama G" lasted the longest. She was my mother-in-law, Anita Martinez Gonzalez, and the matriarch of the Gonzalez family. Not only did we share a passion for education, but we also shared a passion for adventure, especially adventure found through traveling.

I'll never forget her fun-loving spirit when she traveled with our family to Costa Rica and to London on two of the student trips we led. In 2006, at the age of seventy-eight, she learned that Analise, who was in Australia studying at Barker College for a semester, would be spending Easter alone. She wouldn't have it. Even though *Abuela's* numerous travels had already taken her to Australia, she boarded a plane and endured the arduous seventeen-hour plane ride to ensure that Analise would have company for Easter. Remembering Analise's love for Tex-Mex, she even made Analise a pan of her award-winning enchiladas.

At the age of eighty, Mama G. decided to travel once again to China to see how it had changed since she first had seen China at age fifty. And then at the ripe age of eighty-two, she joined us one weekend at our cabin in Arkansas. When I asked her if she wanted to go on an ATV ride with me, her quick response was, "Of course!"

She held on to me tightly as we rode through the mountain trails around our cabin. After I made a pretty sharp turn, I turned to her and yelled, "Are you okay?"

"I could do this all day!"

Mama G. was a force of nature and a pioneer among Mexican-American women. She valued her faith, her family, and her education most. She taught history to fifth- and sixth-graders until the age of seventy-two when she finally and reluctantly decided that she probably should retire.

She was a beautiful, strong, energetic woman who prided herself in her appearance; she always looked twenty years younger than her age. And she was a natural leader and role model for many in her church, school, and large extended family.

When I married into her family, I instantly had a large family that I cherished and that my children were able to spend every major holiday with—a gift that as a child, I always wanted. Clearly, when my children's *abuela* passed away in 2014, there was a big hole left in the Gonzalez family.

After her estate is settled, we decide that one of the best ways we could honor Mama G's spirit is to take a family trip together. Our family has already grown quite a bit since Scott had said "My family is now you" in his wedding vows. Not only do we have two grown, fully launched children to accompany us on our trip, but we also have Sally, our beautiful second daughter whom David has married, and our first grandchild, precious Porter. Analise is happily engaged to a wonderful young man from Denver who has a very special name: Charlie. He will join us, too.

We arrive at Treasure Island from three states—Texas, Arkansas, and Colorado. I've found a cozy beach cottage to rent; when we get there we learn that it originally was Babe Ruth's summer house. For four days, the seven of us spend time making memories in the water, on the sand, and around the table at mealtimes. It is a priceless blessing to be together as a family—yes, the family I always dreamed of having.

July 2017

The older I get, the harder it is to look in the mirror. Now at the age of sixty, whenever I see my face, I can't help but see my receding hairline—one that looks so much like my mom's had looked in her later years. It's not enough that I have her hanging stomach; now I even have her receding hairline.

Since I've hit middle age, along with my loss of hormones, I've also lost more than half of my hair. It's one thing to be a bald male and to be considered sexy but quite another to be a female with thinning hair and to be considered unattractive.

For the last fifteen years, I've tried everything to grow more hair. Nothing has worked. Even though I've always considered myself like Carole King to be a "natural woman," in desperation one day I went to one of the most expensive wig shops in Dallas and was fit by an expert for a beautiful wig. I even bravely wore it to a wedding, but when two of my close friends didn't initially recognize me, I donated the wig to a non-profit.

One day when whining to my friend Suzette about my hair loss, she asks if I've ever thought about getting a weave. I haven't. Now, the more I think about it, if my hair loss is affecting my self-esteem this much, maybe I should try a weave.

I find a highly reviewed studio that's owned by a woman from Cameroon named Brittany. When I call Brittany and tell her about my hair loss, she assures me that she has done weaves for many women like me.

A few days later, she meets me at the door of her studio. Her compassion quickly wins me over, as do the before-and-after pictures of women with alopecia whom she's helped.

First, I'll need to choose natural hair that she'll dye to the color of my liking. I select a slightly curly shoulder-length blend that costs $350; it should last through a year's worth of weaves. I'll also have to pay her $300 for the approximate four-hour process of weaving the new hair into my existing hair. But the high cost of getting a weave is worth it if it can ensure an increase in my self-esteem.

A week later, I venture back to Brittany's hair studio.

She greets me with a big smile and asks, "Are you ready?"

Since I'm already in so deep, I know there is only one right answer: "Yes."

I look around her studio and notice that I'm the only one there who isn't African American. We walk to a small room in the back of her studio.

First, Brittany braids my hair into tight cornrows—something I've wanted to have done since 1979 when Bo Derek stepped out of the water in the movie *Ten.* Since my hair is so sparse, Brittany braids extra thread into each braid. I feel pulling all over my head. She tells me that this is normal, and Advil will help.

After making the cornrows, Brittany attaches a net to my head, and then she begins to sew the net to each cornrow. More pulling is involved—so much so, that when I see myself in the mirror, I look about twenty years younger due to all the wrinkles that are pulled back from my forehead!

Finally, Brittany threads two big needles and tells me she will sew each piece of my new hair into the net and cornrows. The process is painstaking and painful, but it's wonderful to see a new me unfold—a woman who finally has the hair she wishes she had been born with.

Janis joins me in the middle of the process and keeps me laughing. Despite the pain from all the pulling, it's worth it when I look at the new me smiling into the mirror.

After three-and-half hours of standing on her feet, Brittany completes her work. What a work of art it is! Unfortunately, it's a masterpiece with a life expectancy of only six to eight weeks; in a couple of months, I'll have to go through this laborious process all over again.

After we leave the studio, Janis and I decide to celebrate with dinner, but I find it difficult to eat because my head is hurting so much.

Five hours later, I finally arrive back home and slowly walk into the den to reveal my new hairstyle to Scott. He looks up from a book he's been reading.

"You look great, Christine. Do you like it?"

"I'm still trying to get used to it. I can't believe how much younger I look, but that's because my wrinkles have all been pulled away. My head is hurting so much, and the Advil isn't helping."

"I bet you'll feel better in the morning."

An hour later, we get into bed. Within a few minutes, I realize that I'm sleeping on a thickly tied, bumpy mat-of-a-head. I keep trying to find a comfy place to rest my head, but after tossing and turning ceaselessly, I realize no spot can be found. The pain continues, and nothing can be done about it. Since I've spent so much time and money on this process, I know I can't whine to Scott; I simply must endure.

Because I haven't slept much, I'm grumpy when I wake the next morning, and my head is still throbbing. Since I'm preparing for a trip on the following day to visit my East Coast family, we have some important errands to run.

As we drive on errand after errand, my head continues to hurt, and I'm having a tough time functioning. By lunchtime, Scott can tell I'm not feeling like myself and asks if I'm okay. I must come clean.

"Scott, I'm still in so much pain. I didn't get much sleep, either, because I couldn't get comfortable all night. The Advil hasn't done a thing. I'm so worried about leaving for New Jersey and being in this much pain. What should I do?"

"I don't know, Christine. You need to make the decision. Whatever you decide, I'll support you."

After thinking a bit more, I realize the only way I can find relief from my pain is for the weave to be taken out.

I'm too embarrassed to call Brittany. My only hope is that Janis, who was there when it went in, could somehow use her great talent as a seamstress to remove it. I call her, and despite her living forty-five minutes from our home, she says she'll be right over.

The process of removing the weave is extremely tedious as it involves careful cutting and unwrapping, but with both Janis and Scott's assistance, the weave comes out in a third of the time it took to be put in.

As Janis begins to unbraid the cornrows closest to my forehead, she remarks, "You poor girl! No wonder why you have been in so much pain!"

As the last tiny braid is unbraided, and I'm left with my forehead wrinkles and skimpy, frizzy hair, I look in the mirror and feel truly blessed. While I have alopecia, I still have hair, and every strand of it is a gift from my Maker.

I turn to thank Scott and Janis.

Tears are forming in Scott's eyes as I hear him ask Janis, "How can we get this woman to know that she is beautiful and loved just the way she is?"

August 2017

What Life Has Taught Me

For my children and grandchildren

1. Balance is best in all things.
2. To everything there is a season.
3. Often, "in theory" and "in practice" are two very different things.
4. Happiness often comes from having few expectations.
5. It takes so little to make someone's day.
6. Show up.
7. Givers are so much happier than takers.
8. Never stop learning.
9. Do the right thing, even if you don't feel like doing it and it's inconvenient.
10. Thank God for your many blessings each day.
11. Keep an open mind. There are many right answers to just about everything.
12. Sometimes being kind is more important than being right.
13. Never stop believing in what you can grow to be.
14. Forgive, cause if you don't, it will hurt you more than it hurts them.
15. Travel not to escape life, but for life not to escape you.
16. Pray. We don't know how it works, but if nothing else, it helps us.
17. There are many flavors of faith and many ways to find God.
18. You marry in infatuated love and stay married on committed love.
19. Loyalty is one of the most underrated virtues.
20. When in doubt, go outside in nature and look up.
21. Never stop celebrating the highs in life
22. Listen to as many different types of music as often as you can.

23. When on a long road trip, find ways to enjoy the journey as much as the destination.
24. God never promised us protection, but He did promise us support.
25. If you get, give; if you learn, teach.
26. If you don't use it, you'll lose it; exercise your body and mind daily.
27. Pick up trash whenever you see it.
28. You can't understand a person until you have walked in his/her shoes or heard his/her story. Ask for that story.
29. Don't wait to be invited...invite.
30. I'd rather spend my life living like there is a God and learn afterwards that I was wrong, than spend my life living like there isn't a God and learn afterwards that I was wrong.

December 2017
Age 60

Your tail is still wagging
even though you fell when getting on our bed
We both have fallen this year
and felt frail and old
but you have me beat
cause dog years mean so much more.

Each day your breathing is more labored
You can't hear much or see well
Your hips keep slipping and
your legs often collapse
A nasty cough has begun and
your big heart is slowly giving out.

I spent my fifties with you by my side
You filled my empty nest as we
hiked to the river and up mountains
You swam in your pond and chased
rocks sinking into the river
You never stopped licking our feet.

And today after sharing more
sweet moments than seem possible
just a few hours of your life remain.

Even in the end
we never stopped giving you
the love you deserve
and you never stopped
loving us in return

January 2018

Last month we made one of the toughest decisions of our lives. In September, Argie, our beloved "third child," was diagnosed with congestive heart failure and started to have coughing fits. He coughed like this because his lungs were filling up with fluid, and he would eventually suffocate as he would not be able to breathe.

Scott and I had always told each other that we would never let Argie suffer at the end of his life. We wanted him to have the kind of death that we, in our wildest dreams, want: one on our own terms where we would pass gently and without pain into God's loving arms. Regrettably, it isn't easy for humans to have this kind of passing. But thankfully, we were able to provide this type of death for our beloved dog.

Dr. Erika from Lap of Love came to our home and looked at our Argie pictures and listened to our Argie stories as we stroked him and told him our thank-yous. We could tell that Argie understood, just like he always had, exactly what was going on. After our poignant farewell, Argie passed on to Doggie Heaven in our bed—the bed he always had found refuge in. I was not emotionally equipped to be there for the final shot that stopped his heart. And then Scott lovingly carried Argie's body out to Dr. Erika's car.

My emptiness began.

Argie had been by my side every day for almost fourteen years. During this time, I had spent more hours with him than with any human; he knew me in ways that nobody else did. This loss was greater than any loss I'd experienced since Daddy had passed in 1990. And my psyche felt it.

Thankfully, we had planned an after-Christmas trip to Spain and Portugal; for a while, our focus shifted, as traveling still exhilarated us like few things could. But as it got closer to our arrival back to the United States, we both began to imagine what it would be like to return to our home after a trip and not to find Argie there waiting for us. It was simply too difficult to think about, and it was impossible to emotionally prepare for; some things just are.

We arrived home, and I've been an emotional wreck since then. I've cried many times throughout each day, and tonight, no matter what I tell myself about the happy, long life Argie lived and how he was so spoiled by us, I still cannot find solace. I miss him. He provided me with unconditional companionship and comfort. It doesn't matter how full my life is with my husband, my children and their families, my career, my friends, my church work, and my non-profit; still, a great emptiness remains.

An hour ago, I had a panic attack—my first in many years. I called out to Scott, and he came right away. This time I didn't think I was having a heart attack, and we didn't rush to the emergency room. Rather, when Scott asked what he could do to help me, I told him to just sit next to me without judgment. I felt equipped this time to ride through my storm of panic. I slowly breathed in and breathed out. I walked around our home but didn't leave it in fear like I had done in the past. And I prayed that this feeling would pass, and eventually it did.

And This is Now
So grateful; So blessed
Summer 2019

I now realize that there is much more to this memoir than just recounting the details of my traumatic childhood—what I often heard my daddy tell me that I would someday do. Regrettably, millions of children endure years filled with trauma. According to Dr. Robert Block, the former President of the American Academy of Pediatrics, "Adverse childhood experiences are the single greatest unaddressed public health threat facing our nation today."

According to a 2019 survey of more than 144,000 adults from twenty-five states, a report from the Centers for Disease Control and Prevention found that almost 60 percent of Americans had at least one adverse experience during their childhoods, and 15.6 percent had experienced four or more different types. The more types of adverse childhood experiences, or ACEs, a person has endured, the higher his or her risk is for negative outcomes. The survey measured these types of childhood adversity: physical, sexual, or verbal abuse; physical and emotional neglect; having an alcoholic or drug addicted parent or one who is diagnosed with mental illness; witnessing a mother who experiences abuse; losing a parent to abandonment, divorce, or death; and having a family member in jail.

I suspect that most of these children, like me, will never be able to forget their trauma or to avoid being affected by their adverse experiences; they simply can't "get over it" like so many people tell them to do. Childhood trauma is not something you just get over.

When you experience trauma in your childhood, no matter how hard you try to shove it under the carpet and pretend that you are done dealing with it, later in life it is still there. Like a turtle hiding in its shell, trauma slowly peeks its head out, often when you least expect, and says, "Thought I was gone, did you? I'm still here. Deal with me again."

Since I left my mother's house at the early age of fourteen and finally was able to get out of her presence for most of each year, I've tried hard to convince others that this turtle doesn't exist, or if she does exist, I've struggled to keep her head inside her shell. And I've also tried to never let anyone who meets me think to themselves, "Like mother, like daughter." For the most part, it has worked.

Medical research further reveals that the negative effects of adverse childhood experiences change children in ways that can endure in their bodies for decades. Prior to writing "Lifelong Impacts of Childhood Trauma," Dr. Vincent Filetti, chief of Kaiser Permanente's Department of Preventive Medicine, and Dr. Bob Anda, research scientist at the Centers for Disease Control and Prevention studied over 17,000 adults—70 percent of whom were Caucasian and college educated—and found that traumatic childhood experiences play out powerfully even fifty years after they occurred.

In her 2014 TEDMED talk, "How Childhood Trauma can make you a Sick Adult," pediatrician Nadine Burke Harris' addressed Filetti and Anda's study and the dose/response relationship between adverse childhood experiences and health outcomes. Harris described how the repeated stress of abuse, neglect, or parents struggling with mental health or substance abuse issues has real, tangible effects on the development of a child's brain and body. As a result, children who experience high levels of trauma are at triple the risk for developing serious adult diseases like heart disease and lung cancer and are over four times more likely to suffer from depression; consequently, it is crucial that those who have experienced childhood trauma get counseling and medical help as quickly as possible.

So how has this research played out in my life? I doubt it's a coincidence that since my childhood, I have had fourteen medical procedures or surgeries. Children who have endured adverse childhood experiences are also more prone to accidents. As I write this, I'm recovering from yet another painful surgery caused by yet another accidental fall. Since 2013, I've fallen five times.

My recent fall occurred when I was walking our foster labradoodle on slippery mud, and she lurched at a nearby workman. All four tendons of my rotator cuff tore; I never have been one to do anything half-assed.

More than anything, right now I'm working on moving mindfully and being grounded. When I'm grounded, I'm planted so deeply that nothing can uproot me. I'm focusing on the now, not worrying about the future. I feel safe. I have health. I'm at peace.

Childhood trauma also often leads a person to crave security and to hold on to objects or behaviors much longer than what is usually thought to be normal. For me, it meant sucking on a bottle till I was in kindergarten, sucking my thumb till I spent my first night sleeping next to a man, and bringing my pillow with a crisp pillowcase to flick whenever I travel. I still crave *hygge*, the Danish word for a cozy environment that engenders well-being. I always try to sit in corners in restaurants, and each night I sleep with a weighted blanket. I doubt I will ever outgrow my need to feel secure.

When you grow up in a house with a person who is often out of control, you learn to value situations you *can* control. And when life brings you situations that you can't control—like what a puppy does to your home or backyard when you're away, or when someone you love is diagnosed with a life-threatening disease, or when you face overwhelming demands from a new administration at your workplace—anxiety is just a breath away.

At these times, I'm taken right back to 97 Rumford Road, to the church services where I anxiously sat with my stomach in knots waiting to see if my mother would speak out, and to my fifth-grade classroom where my mentally deranged mother suddenly appeared. I feel the horror once again, and anxiety seizes my body.

Last year, I read the sweet story of a ninety-four-year-old woman who just had married her ninety-five-year-old boyfriend. When asked the secret to their longevity, she quickly responded, "We do not let things that we can't control bother us in the least." This is how I want to live the remainder of my life.

Additionally, I continue to work on being kind to myself by taking better care of my body; as I learned with Marty Glass, this means that I must make choices and practice habits that honor it. James Clear, in his groundbreaking book *Atomic Habits* writes that the most effective way to change habits is not by focusing on what you want to achieve; instead, focus on whom you wish to become. Every act of kindness that I show myself is a vote for the type of person I wish to become. Eventually, the more I practice habits that align with the vision of myself I desire, the more readily I will override the negative effects of my childhood trauma.

I've also learned that I can wear an invisible backpack of tools so I'll be equipped to deal with my anxiety when it strikes. But first, I must know what triggers my anxiety and work hard to avoid these stress-producing situations. If the triggers are unavoidable, as flying through turbulence on an airplane often is, then I'll initiate the relaxation responses I've learned to practice. Besides knitting, I've learned self-regulation techniques that are always available in my invisible backpack; doing slow, deep breathing and listening to calming music are two of these techniques. I'm still learning what works best for me as I'll inevitably continue to face situations that are seemingly out of my control—situations that quickly bring my trauma turtle out of her shell.

What I know for sure is that I haven't done this work alone. Since I left home, I've had many teachers who have taught me ways to lessen my anxiety disorder. The prayers and support of my daddy and of countless others have buffered the trauma of my childhood. Through my large support system, I've learned resilience that has enabled me not only to survive but also to thrive.

Without Scott by my side when I've woken in the middle of the night thinking I was having a heart attack; the times I've gone to the emergency room, only to learn that once again, it was a false alarm;

the times I've been terrified during airplane turbulence; the times when I needed to know that Scott was just a text or a phone call away, I doubt I would have had wings to fly so high. My soul sister Janis and other close friends have supplemented Scott's support. One can't do the tough work of dealing with the effects of childhood trauma alone.

But even with this great support, I am still left with a choice. Do I live the remainder of my life focusing on my traumatic childhood, or do I move past it and focus on what I've learned from it and how this knowledge can help others? My inspiring yoga therapist, Trionne Barnett, recently reinforced this important lesson—one that can be applied to any negative circumstance that arises in my life. Rather than asking "Why me?" I need to ask myself "What for?"

Ultimately, I have learned that I have the power to overcome the effects of my childhood trauma.

While I don't have the power to control the unexpected anxiety triggers that will continue to arise, I do have the power to frame them as messengers from Above that will teach me and hopefully contribute to my growth. I want my life to be a grain of sand that doesn't merely lie on the beach; I want it to slip into an oyster and to be a catalyst for God's work to begin and become.

Looking Ahead

> *The final stage of healing is using what happens to you to help other people.*—Gloria Steinem

I'm so grateful to each of you who has taken the time to read my story. So now, what about yours?

If you are one of the hundreds of millions who also experienced trauma in your childhood, I hope that my memoir gives you hope that you, too, can find ways to overcome its effects in whatever form it has manifested itself in your life. It is never too late to heal.

In addition to talking to a counselor who is trained to help individuals who have experienced traumatic childhoods, you may also find valuable information from these resources:

Books:

Bevan-Lee, Donna. *Iron Legacy: Childhood Trauma and Adult Transformation*. Seattle: Bevan-Lee Publishing, 2019.

Burke Harris, Nadine. *The Deepest Well: Healing the Long-Term Effects of Childhood Adversity*. New York: Houghton Mifflin Harcourt, 2019.

Karr-Morse, R. and Wiley, M.S. *Scared Sick: The Role of Childhood Trauma in Adult Disease*. New York: Basic Books, 2012.

Nakazawa, Donna J. Childhood Disrupted: *How Your Biography Becomes Your Biology and How You Can Heal*. New York: Simon and Schuster, Inc., 2015.

Van der Kolk, B. A. (2014). *The Body Keeps the Score: Brain, Mind, and Body in the Healing of Trauma*. New York: Penguin Random House, 2014.

Walker, Pete. Complex PTSD: *From Surviving to Thriving*. Contra Costa: Azure Coyote, 2013.

Organizations:

American Academy of Child and Adolescent Psychiatry
www.aacap.org

Anna Institute
www.theannainstitute.org

American Professional Society on the Abuse of Children
www.apsac.org

Child Trauma Academy
www.childtrauma.org

The National Center for Trauma-Informed Care
www.nasddds.org

The National Child Traumatic Stress Network
www.nctsn.org

National Trauma Consortium
www.nationaltraumaconsortium.org

Overcome Anxiety Project
www.overcomeanxietyproject.org

The Trauma Stewardship Institute
www.traumastewardship.com

Acknowledgments

For reading this manuscript in its early stages and sharing your thoughts on how I could improve it, I owe deep gratitude to Janis Dworkis, Theresa Eichenwald, Barb Frost, Gene Frost, Scott Gonzalez, Socorro Gonzalez, Analise Gonzalez-Fine, Roberta (Bobbi) Mailer, Elsie Nicolette, Paul Nicolette, Karen Simmons, and David Gonzalez Soames.

Finally, I owe my deepest gratitude to:

- Marie, Ruth Ann, Martha, Mary Ellen, and Anita, my surrogate mothers, who throughout my journey helped me see that there is a better way.
- Paul, my brother, who was there for me then and still is here for me now.
- Janis, my soul sister, whose love carried me when Daddy's no longer could.
- Scott, my life love, whose unconditional love and support brought me home.

Questions for Thought and Discussion

1. According to the memoir, what consequences can an overly zealous religious home life have on a child?
2. What are the manifestations of childhood trauma that Christine faces throughout her life?
3. What contributes to Christine's realization that she is "coming of age?" What occurs during these important years of her life?
4. Discuss the roles Christine's mother's curse, *kina hora*, and superstition play in the memoir.
5. What can be done with the many "Sophies" in our society? Was Charlie ethically correct in allowing Sophie to come home so soon from the hospital on so many occasions?
6. What can be learned from Christine and Paul about the common inequity between siblings when it comes to the caregiving of parents? How does their relationship change throughout the memoir?
7. Clearly, this memoir teaches about the importance of getting help to deal with childhood trauma. Who are the most important people who support Christine? What do they do?
8. What role does living "in a Christian bubble" serve in Christine's life? What role does "being in the world" serve in her growth?
9. Where and how is a home created again and again in the memoir? Why is it so important for Christine to create a home?
10. What causes Christine's self-esteem to be lowered? What causes it to rise?
11. According to the memoir, is God real and does prayer work in Christine's life? When does/doesn't prayer work for her?
12. Discuss the issue of discrimination and how it played out in the memoir. Do you agree with the family members who changed their names? Why or why not?
13. What are some of the coping mechanisms and different ways Christine and her family members deal with the adversity of Sophie's mental illness?

14. Discuss the many location changes that Christine and her family members make. When does a "geographical fix" work and not work? According to the memoir, when does running from a problem work and not work?
15. According to the memoir, what are some ways that the effects of childhood trauma can be alleviated?
16. What are some of the positive outcomes in Christine's life due to the effects of her childhood trauma?
17. Ultimately, how does Christine overcome many of the negative effects of her childhood trauma? What is she still working on today?
18. How does poetry writing, letter writing, and journal writing contribute to Christine's life journey? Can it contribute to yours?